501
GREAT SCRAPBOOK
PAGE IDEAS

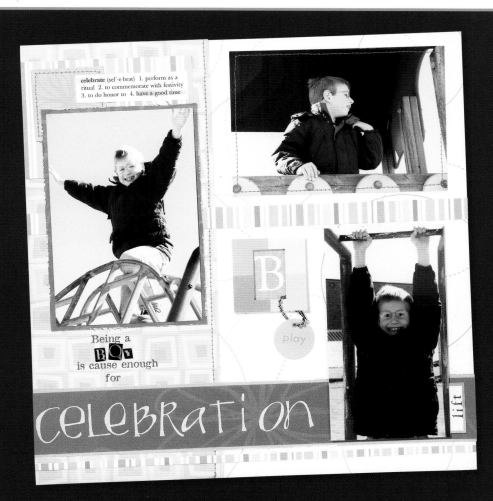

A gallery of themes and inspiration from A to Z

MEMORY
MAKERS
BOOKS

Editors Lydia Rueger, Kerry Arquette

Art Director Nick Nyffeler

Graphic Designers Robin Rozum, Andrea Zocchi

Art Acquisitions Editor Janetta Abucejo Wieneke

Craft Editor Jodi Amidei

Photographer Ken Trujillo

Contributing Photographers Lizzy Creazzo, Jennifer Reeves

Contributing Writers Heather A. Eades, Michelle Pesce

Editorial Support Karen Cain, Emily Curry Hitchingham,
MaryJo Regier, Dena Twinem

Contributing Memory Makers Masters Valerie Barton, Jodi Heinen, Jeniece Higgins, Julie Johnson, Kelli Noto, Heidi Schueller,
Torrey Scott, Trudy Sigurdson, Shannon Taylor, Samantha Walker

Publisher Bob Kaslik

Memory Makers® *501 Great Scrapbook Page Ideas*

Published by Memory Makers Books, an imprint of F+W Publications, Inc.

12365 Huron Street, Suite 500, Denver, CO 80234

Phone (800) 254-9124

First edition. Printed in China

10 09 08 07 06   8 7 6 5 4

Library of Congress Cataloging-in-Publication Data

501 great scrapbook page ideas : a gallery of themes and inspiration from A to Z /
   (editors, Kerry Arquette, Lydia Rueger ; contributing writers, Heather A. Eades, Michelle
Pesce).-- 1st ed.
      p cm.
   Includes bibliographical references and index.
   ISBN 13: 978-1-892127-52-5
   ISBN 10: 1-892127-52-0
   1. Photograph albums. 2. Photographs--Conversation and restoration. 3. Scrapbooks. I.
Title: Five hundred and one great scrapbook page ideas. II. Title: Five hundred one great
scrapbook page ideas. III. Arquette, Kerry. IV. Rueger, Lydia. V. Eades, Heather A. VI.
Pesce, Michelle.

TR465.A1349 2005
745.593--dc22
                                                                          2004066153

Distributed to trade and art markets by

F+W Publications, Inc.

4700 East Galbraith Road, Cincinnati, OH 45236

Phone (800) 289-0963

Memory Makers Books is the home of *Memory Makers,* the scrapbook magazine dedicated to educating and inspiring scrapbookers.
To subscribe, or for more information, call (800) 366-6465.
Visit us on the Internet at www.memorymakersmagazine.com.

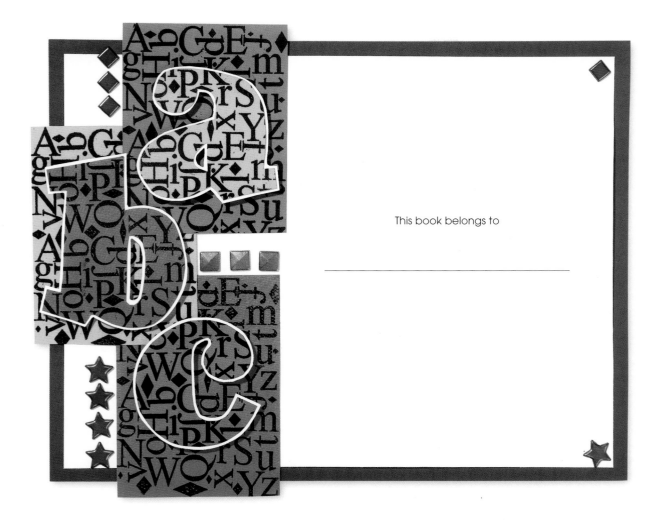

This book belongs to

_____

Dedicated to our many talented contributing artists.
Your continual flow of great page ideas keeps us all inspired.

Torrey Scott, Thornton, Colorado

Supplies: Letter template (C-Thru Ruler); letter stamp (Hampton Art Stamps); shaped brads (Creative Impressions); pumpkin, red, purple, black and white cardstocks; watermark ink; embossing powder; foam tape

Table of Contents

My Cat

cat (kat), n,
soft-furred, litt...
domesticated an...
times or for kil...
pet or for va...
any of the vari...
related to this,
tiger, cougar, l...
3. a person re...
& cat in such

I got Lilly from the Denver Dumb Friends League about a month after moving to Denver in 1998. She was my first present to myself. Occasionally I will remind Derek that Lilly has been around longer than he has. She's now lived in four different homes with me and continues to be a great pet, even after the addition of two dogs.

Lilly

Jodi Amidei, Memory Makers Books
Photos: Lydia Rueger, Memory Makers Books

Supplies: Patterned papers (Bo-Bunny Press, Chatterbox, Karen Foster Design); stamps (Catslife Press, Rubber-stamp Ave., Stampin' Up!); cat charm (American Traditional Designs); collar and letter charm (FAF, Inc.); tag die cut (Sizzix); photo turns (K & Company); ribbons; orange and black cardstocks

Introduction

Memory Makers Book Department: front row (L-R) Janetta Abucejo Wieneke, Robin Rozum, Emily Curry Hitchingham, middle row (L-R) Karen Cain, MaryJo Regier, Lydia Rueger, Jodi Amidei, back row Nick Nyffeler.

If you've been a scrapbooker for more than five minutes, you've probably discovered the dilemma that many face—the endless quest for more ideas on reoccurring topics. Birthdays come once a year, and whether the celebration is big or small, it's rare that a scrapbooker can let one pass without snapping photos from every angle. The same is true for annual summer vacations, sporting events, changing seasons and other occasions on which you won't leave home without your camera. And then there are the simpler yet just as treasured moments of life—children caught in pensive moods, the look on a baby's face as he or she sleeps, those cute expressions that pets make, happy-go-lucky playtime and romantic evenings spent with loved ones. No matter if your photos are lighthearted or serious, energetic or serene, scrapbookers need ideas for all of them. And if there is one thing we've learned from our years in the scrapbooking industry, it's that scrapbookers can never have too much inspiration for the topics they love.

With *501 Great Scrapbook Page Ideas*, we've attempted to quench your thirst for more page ideas in this jampacked 192-page gallery. You'll find a variety of popular topics as well as a few more obscure themes organized from A to Z for quick and easy reference.

And because scrapbookers are always looking for tips to get and stay organized (and because this is the first step to creating great pages), we've included organizational information on page 8. In addition, because smaller, more manageable scrapbook projects are sometimes just what scrapbookers need to re-energize, we've included ideas and fun examples for mini theme albums on page 10.

We hope you enjoy the ideas you'll find throughout this book and will use it again and again for inspiration all throughout the year.

The Staff of Memory Makers Books

Get Organized

Before you begin creating pages on a variety of topics, you'll need to organize your photos. If you see a great idea for a pet page that you'd love to re-create but have no idea where your most recent pet pictures are, you're likely to spend more time searching for photos than creating the page itself! First, decide if you'd like to sort your photos chronologically or by theme. Both are valid systems for photo organization, but the number and type of photos you have to sort may determine which system works best for you. For either method, sort in a spacious area away from direct sunlight where the photos may be spread out for a long period of time in case you can't finish in one sitting. In addition, you'll need to gather archival-quality photo boxes, photo-safe envelopes, a pen and blank self-stick notes before starting.

SORTING PHOTOS CHRONOLOGICALLY

1. Gather photographs from the current year first. The circumstances surrounding these photos will be fresher in your mind and thus the easiest and least intimidating to sort.

2. Remove photos from their original envelopes and place in photo-safe envelopes. Place loose photos in the envelope with pictures that were taken around the same time.

3. Remove photos from their new envelopes temporarily and label each envelope with the events and topics it contains. (Most photo-safe envelopes include blank lines or spaces on the envelope for this purpose.) Be specific but keep your notes brief, including things such as "Daniel's First Birthday" and "Sectional Championship Game." As you label each one, place photos back in their appropriate envelope to avoid mix-ups.

4. Label the envelopes by date and assign each envelope a number. File the envelopes in consecutive numeric order in an archival photo box.

5. Label the photo box with the year or span of months.

SORTING PHOTOS BY THEME

This method of organization works well if you wish to be a little more specific in how you group your photographs or if you have a large number of photos for a single event.

1. Collect all your photos for one large theme at a time (wedding, family, vacations, etc.).

2. On self-stick notes, write down categories that fit the particular theme. Wedding photos, for example, can be sorted into smaller topics such as Rehearsal Dinner, Getting Ready, Ceremony, Reception, Portraits and so on. The same can be done for a standard family album by sorting the photos by holiday events, playtime, home-improvement projects and other themes which feature all family members.

3. Spread out the self-stick notes on a large, empty surface such as a table or the floor. Sort your photos into piles near the appropriate category.

4. Re-sort the photos in each pile so they fall in a logical order. Label photo-safe envelopes by category and place the piles in envelopes. If desired, insert cardstock dividers into the photo box with categories written on them to help you locate specific photos even more quickly. Place all envelopes in a photo storage box and label the box with the date and overall theme.

Jumpstart Your Scrapbooking With Mini Theme Albums

To start creating pages, all you really need are photographs, cardstock, adhesive, a pen and an album. As your style develops, you can add a variety of fun embellishments to enhance your photos such as buttons, ribbon, metallic accents, patterned papers, rubber stamps and more. But as many scrapbookers discover, buying fun supplies and actually getting pages finished are two very different things. Often, creating a mini theme album can be just what a scrapbooker needs to get the creative juices flowing again. And because it's a smaller, more manageable project, it won't take too much time away from your regular family albums. Consider the points on page 11 when creating a theme album:

Jodi Heinen, Sartell, Minnesota

Supplies: Ribbons (Making Memories, Michaels, Offray); rub-on letters, paper clips (Making Memories); letter die cut (Sizzix); conchos (Scrapworks); love charm (source unknown); fabrics; eyelets; brads; green, blue and black cardstocks

• Limit the number of photographs. For mini albums, allow for one photo per spread (unless your photos are really small) in order to have room for your journaling, title and embellishments on each small page.

• Plan and organize content with self-stick notes. After selecting photos, write journaling information, title and order of placement on self-stick notes. Stick one to the back of each photo for reference when creating the pages.

• Keep the topic focused. Don't try to encompass the entire family or all your journaling in a mini theme album. Choose a topic that tends to be glossed over in your standard family albums. Consider themes such as friends, home improvements, all about me or 10 reasons why I love you.

• Choose a layout and keep it consistent. Your album will come together more quickly if you choose a single layout for each small spread and stick to it throughout. As shown on page 10, Jodi Heinen kept the layout of her ABC album simple by including a large letter cut-out on the left-hand side of each spread. Each right-hand page contains a title, one photo, journaling in the same font and fabric embellishment. Jodi saved time by not having to come up with a new layout for each spread, while varying the colors of fabric and ribbon to keep the album bright and interesting.

• Consider a unified color scheme. Choosing a few colors and keeping them the same throughout an album can make it easy to select page supplies. For the friends mini album below, Jeniece Higgins chose a color scheme of pink, cream and brown and carried it throughout her album. While she used a variety of media on her pages (patterned papers, ribbon, charms, stamped letters and metal embellishments), product selection was simplified because she always knew what colors she was looking for.

Jeniece Higgins, Lake Forest, Illinois

Supplies: Album page inserts (Rusty Pickle); patterned papers and letter stamps (Making Memories); tag template, charm and brads (Provo Craft); foam stamps, epoxy letters and bottle cap (Li'l Davis Designs); small letter stamps (Hero Arts); pink paint (Plaid); ribbons; fabric; sewing machine; brown pen

In this book, you'll find:

A is for Animals feathered and furry,

B is for Birthdays that come in a flurry,

And Parts of the Body—below and above,

While C is for Culture and Couples in love.

D is for Dream and the Dirt on kids' faces—

(As well as on hands and most all other places).

E is for Exercise—humans in motion,

And E's for Emotion as broad as the ocean….

F is for Friends and for Flowers that bloom,

As they fill up the world with their fragrant perfume.

Both Goggles and Glasses help all of us see,

And goggles and glasses both start with a G.

Hats can be dapper or ward off the sun,

And so H is for Hats and for Ho-ri-zon,

I is for Insects, for Ice and for snowses,

(Note: Both can cause stinging on vulnerable noses).

J is for Journey and K is for Kites,

L is for Leaves and for Love's soaring heights.

It's said that sweet music can sooth savage beasts,

And so M is for Music on which a beast feasts.

N is for Nature and N is for Name,

O is for Ocean, God's pool filled with rain.

P is for Play and for soul-lifting Prayer,

Q is for Quiet—   (rare).

R's for Remember and also for Rain

That forms puddles for pooches and kids in the lane,

So there's splishing and splashing and brave puddle-leaping,

And tired-out children, so S is for Sleeping.

T is for Teatime all sugar and spice.

And U is for Uh-Oh, those spills that aren't nice.

V is for Vehicle—cars, bikes and trains,

While W gazes out Windowy panes.

X is a letter that's not made for rhyming,

(Attempting to do so would throw off my timing.

And meter's important in every great verse

So an X-letter rhyme is a poet's worst curse.)

Y is for Yell and it's also for Yawn,

Which, coupled with stretching, can welcome the dawn.

Z is for Zoo where guests growl, howl and bray....

Where there's feathers and fur....

... Look! We're back now at "A"!

And just like a poem that starts where it ends,

A scrapbooker's love for both family and friends,

And times that they share shall continue to be,

When they're cherished in albums with themes A-Z.

—*Kerry Arquette*

Jodi Amidei, Memory Makers Books

Supplies: Burgundy, gold, forest green and black cardstocks; animal print fabrics; vellum; eyelets

A is for Animals

an•i•mal (an´i mol) n. any of a kingdom having the ability to move quickly and obtain food, with specialized sense organs

Frog

Shannon's neighbors returned from camping with several dozen baby frogs to release at a nearby lake, and Shannon managed to get one of them to stay on her finger long enough to take a photo—even while changing her camera batteries one-handed! She tinted an old photo of a picnic tabletop for her background and silhouetted the frog on her fingertips in a paint program for a fun layout about the joy of curiosity.

Shannon Freeman, Bellingham, Washington

Supplies: Drawing program (MicroGrafx Draw); image-editing software (Microsoft Photo Editor); paint program (Microsoft Paint)

Goodbye Friend

Maryann used perspective and creative framing to highlight the star of this layout, the turtle, against a background of neighborhood children. Extra landscape photos also found new life as embellishments that help tie the different parts of the layout together.

MaryAnn Wise, The Woodlands, Texas

Supplies: Patterned papers (Carolee's Creations); wood frames (Li'l Davis Designs); white cardstock

Puppy in a Backpack

Heather filed away a cute story about her 3-year-old daughter placing the family puppy in a backpack. She placed her page title made of letter stickers, copper frames, ribbon and label maker tape on top of the tiny file folder that contains the story.

Heather Preckel, Swannanoa, North Carolina

Supplies: Patterned papers (Creative Imaginations, Sweetwater); ribbon (May Arts); letter stickers (Paper Loft, Wordsworth); file folder (Rusty Pickle); copper frames (Nunn Design); charm (Maya Road); label maker (Dymo); brown stamping ink

Big Fish Story

A dramatic enlargement perfectly echoes the "big" theme of this page—big fish, big excitement and big photo! The bottle-cap embellishment complements the page's monochromatic color scheme, and the ribbon adds just a touch of femininity to this little girl's fish story.

Barb Hogan, Cincinnati, Ohio

Supplies: Patterned papers (SEI); letter stickers (Creative Imaginations); bottle cap (Li'l Davis Designs); brown cardstock; ribbon; transparency

How Embarrassing

When Colleen caught her typically photogenic cat looking anything but regal one night, she knew she had the raw materials for a fun digital feline layout. She created her background by using a tile filter twice with a black background and brown foreground, then added some variation by applying a metallic gradient.

Colleen Yoshida, Cold Lake, Alberta, Canada

Supplies: Image-editing software (Adobe Photoshop)

Always Take Time to Smell the Roses

Allowing a long title to frame a photo is an effective way to emphasize a single photo of your favorite furry companion. Christine also created her own "conchos" by punching nested ovals out of metallic paper.

Christine Traversa, Joliet, Illinois

Supplies: Punches (Family Treasures); rose sticker (K & Company); flower stamp (Stampin' Up!); slide mounts (QVC); light blue and tan cardstocks, olive corrugated paper; watermark and brown stamping inks

Puppy Love

Taking a cue from the colors in her photo, Janice's monochromatic layout lets this photo of her curious pup shine. A low-key title, crumpled and inked paper, and a few carefully chosen embellishments add just the right amount of style.

Janice Lund, Windsor, California

Supplies: Patterned paper (Doodlebug Design); rivets (Chatterbox); label holder (Making Memories); letter stickers (Deluxe Designs); brown and tan cardstocks; brown stamping ink; ribbon

Our Newest Addition

Including "then" and "now" photos on the same layout is a wonderful way to chronicle the growth of your pet. Carmel's list of doggie statistics offers a glimpse into her pooch's quirky personality.

Carmel Flores, Westfield, Indiana

Supplies: Patterned papers (7 Gypsies, Paper Adventures); metal frame, heart and brads (Making Memories); letter stamps (All Night Media); sticker letters (Colorbök); punch (McGill); brown, black and tan cardstocks; vellum

Buddies Forever

There is something beautifully unique about the relationship between a child and his dog, which Laura captures in her focal-point photograph and the heartfelt journaling beneath it. To make the hinge for the focal-point photo, she used eyelets instead of buttons in a strip of button holes, then ran twine through them and anchored the ends with decorative brads.

Laura McKinley, Westport, Connecticut

Supplies: Patterned papers (Chatterbox); stickers (Bo-Bunny Press, EK Success, Paper Loft, Sweetwater); decorative brads and date stamp (Making Memories); brown cardstock; brown stamping ink; twine; black and tan eyelets

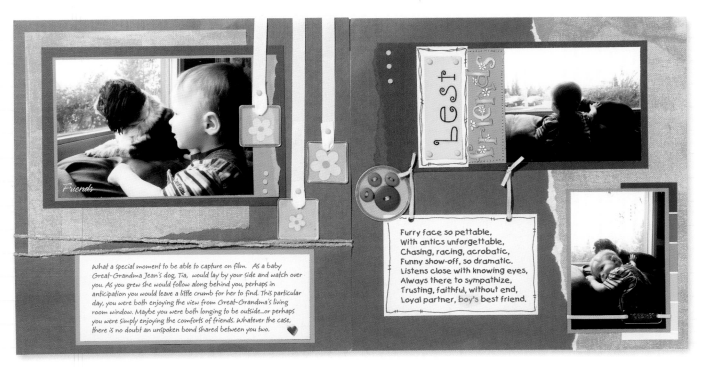

> What a special moment to be able to capture on film. As a baby Great-Grandma Jean's dog, Tia, would lay by your side and watch over you. As you grew she would follow along behind you, perhaps in anticipation you would leave a little crumb for her to find. This particular day, you were both enjoying the view from Great-Grandma's living room window. Maybe you were both longing to be outside...or perhaps you were simply enjoying the comforts of friends. Whatever the case, there is no doubt an unspoken bond shared between you two.

> Furry face so pettable,
> With antics unforgettable,
> Chasing, racing, acrobatic,
> Funny show-off, so dramatic.
> Listens close with knowing eyes,
> Always there to sympathize,
> Trusting, faithful, without end,
> Loyal partner, boy's best friend.

Best Friends

Aimee filled her journaling with the small details that capture the relationship between a dog and her son. A paint chip adds subtle pizazz as a partial mat for one photo.

Aimee Grenier, Hinton, Alberta, Canada

Supplies: Patterned paper (Mustard Moon); vellum tags, rub-on word and heart brad (Making Memories); letters (Beary Patch); metal word tag and sticker (Colorbök); flower stickers (Karen Foster Design); letter stickers (Provo Craft); blue, green and cream cardstocks; buttons; thread; brads; eyelets; ribbon; chalk; paint chip; twill ribbon; fibers

Roadside Friends

Barb was so charmed by a pack of horses along an oft traveled road that she set out with a camera and carrots in hand to capture her "friends." Her paper choices, fonts and distressing give the page a distinct Old West feel.

Barb Hogan, Cincinnati, Ohio

Supplies: Patterned papers (Daisy D's, K & Company); black and tan cardstocks; black stamping ink; fibers

The Wild Ponies

What better showcase for photos of wild horses than a layout that looks wild and natural itself? Kristen mimicked natural elements with neutral crumpled and inked papers, different types of mesh and a rolled cardstock stick.

Kristen Swain, Bear, Delaware

Supplies: Letter and tag templates (Scrap Pagerz); letter stamps (Hero Arts); black, olive and tan cardstocks; mesh; brads; chalk; jute; brown stamping ink

Off Leash

Not only do Robin's daily forays to the off leash park give her dog a chance to run like a maniac, they give Robin a chance to clear her head and keep herself in power-walking shape. She trapped stone beads between a piece of page protector sewn to corrugated paper to create a unique, rugged frame for her focal-point photo.

Robin Bell, Calgary, Alberta, Canada

Supplies: Patterned papers and die cuts (Provo Craft); stickers (Colorbök, Me & My Big Ideas); circle tags (Stampin' Up!); metallic rub-ons (Craf-T); beads; linen thread; ball chain; chalk; clear lacquer; paper clay

A Pony Called Lady

Create a layout as unique as your favorite four-legged family member by decorating background papers with acrylic paints and metallic rub-ons. Painting on crumpled cardstock adds additional pizazz and texture without detracting from the photo.

Maria Williams, Cary, North Carolina

Supplies: Letter stickers (EK Success, K & Company, Making Memories); bookplate (7 Gypsies); metallic powder (Jacquard Products); metallic rub-ons (Craf-T); white and black cardstocks; ribbon; acrylic paint; transparency; charm; brown stamping ink

July 2003

There is nothing cuter than small children and animals, and the center photo on this layout qualifies on both counts. Cherie constructed an eye-catching background by crumpling and inking strips of patterned paper and cardstock, then sewing them to her layout.

Cherie Ward, Colorado Springs, Colorado

Supplies: Patterned papers (Chatterbox, Karen Foster Design, Mustard Moon, Rusty Pickle); flower die cuts (Leeco); library label (7 Gypsies); washer eyelets and metal-rimmed tags (Creative Impressions); Mother Goose tag (K & Company); cream, orange and pink cardstocks; metal-rimmed tags; ribbon; black stamping ink; transparency; thread; eyelets; watercolor crayons

Piglet's Big Movie

A child's first movie experience is a pop culture rite of passage, and a tender moment captured between child and stuffed pig is the perfect accompaniment for this story. Nora re-created the look of the movie's title with a combination of handcut letters and letter stickers.

Nora Noll, Glastonbury, Connecticut

Supplies: Patterned paper (Paper Fever); letter stickers (Me & My Big Ideas); pink cardstocks; black stamping ink; date stamp; flower eyelets

Cherish

The tattered nature of Heather's layout brings to mind the story of the Velveteen Rabbit...or in this case, her daughter's favorite stuffed bear. For a look as unique as her daughter's cherished companion, Heather cut one photo into three parts and adhered a transparency printed with her journaling over the center piece.

Heather Uppencamp, Provo, Utah

Supplies: Patterned papers (Daisy D's, Rusty Pickle); title and definition (Making Memories); olive cardstock; walnut ink; chalks; lace; transparency; thread

Winter Joy

An understated, monochromatic color scheme highlights this amazing bird photo taken in one of Marsha's favorite places. She used decoupage glue to decorate plain slide mounts with glitter and tiny silver stars, echoing the shimmering effect of snow in the sunshine.

Marsha Phillips, North Tonawanda, New York
Photos: David Phillips, North Tonawanda, New York

Supplies: Patterned paper (Stampin' Up!); white netting (PSX Design); blue mesh (Magenta); letter stickers (C-Thru Ruler); snowflake stickers and snowflake punch (EK Success); gray, slate blue, blue, light blue and white cardstocks; blue and glitter vellum; mulberry paper; fibers; eyelets; snowflake punch; slide mounts; silver glitter and stars; decoupage glue; bird feather; foam tape

Cardinals

Missy's photos pay tribute to the cardinal while showcasing the differences in coloring between the male and female birds. She continued the woodsy, natural feel of her photographs by using sticklike clips made of bamboo, barklike handmade papers and mesh to accent her title.

Missy Partridge, Berlin, Maryland

Supplies: Patterned paper and textured papers (Provo Craft); mesh strip and bamboo clips (7 Gypsies); letter die cuts (QuicKutz); cream and black cardstocks; red and brown stamping inks; ribbon; brads; tag

The Yearling

First came the dream of owning horses and then the decision to try to breed their own foal. As this special colt reached his first birthday, Kathlene created a layout to celebrate the milestone. She sanded the edges of her photos with an Emory board and then inked them to create a softly framed, rustic look.

Kathlene Clark, Placerville, California

Supplies: Patterned papers (K & Company, Scenic Route Paper Co.); photo anchors, label holder and deco brads (Making Memories); wood letters (Li'l Davis Designs); premade letters (source unknown); letter stamps (Hero Arts); green, brown and tan cardstocks; vellum; paint; brads; brown stamping ink

Jasmine

Karen gave a photo of her pooch artistic flair by applying a paint effect with image-editing software then printing it out on textured cardstock to resemble painted canvas. Painted and sanded metal borders complement the art gallery look while floral papers and ribbon bring out the femininity of this classy canine.

Karen Robinson, Cumberland, Rhode Island

Supplies: Patterned paper (Me & My Big Ideas); letter templates (Scrap Pagerz, Wordsworth); silk flower, metal border accents, decorative brads, date stamp and staples (Making Memories); mini paper bag (www.memoriesoftherabbit.com); light green, white and red cardstocks; white chalk stamping ink; ribbon; eyelets; acrylic paint; thread

Good Ole Clyd

A stamped and inked dog tag makes the perfect embellishment for this dog page. By punching extra photos into squares, Sam was able to include a variety of photos featuring different aspects of Clyd's personality.

Sam Cole, Stillwater, Minnesota

Supplies: Patterned papers and suede letters (EK Success); dog print stamp (Stamp Craft); letter stamps (Hero Arts); dog tag (Making Memories); dark green, olive and brown cardstocks; ball chain; square punch; black stamping ink; brads; foam tape

A Boy and His Own Dog

Sam muses about the relationship between a boy and his dog next to a photo of the two hunting companions. The title itself becomes the main embellishment on the page through the use of different lettering styles and media.

Sam Cole, Stillwater, Minnesota

Supplies: Patterned paper (EK Success, Karen Foster Design); letter stickers (Creative Imaginations, Colorbök, EK Success, Making Memories); leather tag (Rusty Pickle); stamps (EK Success, Stamp Craft); dark green and olive cardstocks; black stamping ink; circle punches; twine

Peacocks of Ruthin Castle

Carolyn couldn't bring an actual peacock feather home with her from Wales, so its vibrant colors became the inspiration for her layout. A tag collaged with fibers, beads, stickers, cording and mesh serves as the backdrop for an exquisite iron-on feather appliqué.

Carolyn Cleveland, Maysville, Georgia

Supplies: Patterned papers and stickers (Club Scrap); beads (www.alltheextras.com); iron-on appliqués (Hirschberg Schutz & Co.); mesh (Magic Mesh); navy, blue, turquoise and white cardstocks; eyelet; fibers; wire

Smores

Cork, corduroy, a silk flower and a metal buckle give this page almost as much color, texture and dimension as Smores the guinea pig himself. Shannon coated the title in clear lacquer to give it more emphasis and a high-gloss shine.

Shannon Taylor, Bristol, Tennessee

Supplies: Patterned papers, cork tag, silk flower and letter stickers (Rusty Pickle); buckle (Junkitz); clear lacquer (JudiKins); brown and black cardstocks; ribbon; corduroy fabric; brads; foam tape

B is for Body Parts

bod•y (bäd é) n. the whole physical structure and substance of a human being, animal or plant
part (pärt) n. a portion or division of a whole

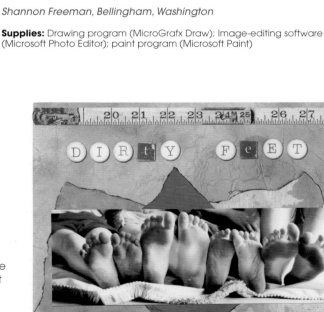

Perfect Pieces of You

Stephanie created a custom patterned transparency with a variety of fonts and her printer. She brushed acrylic paint on patterned paper to tone down the intensity of the color, allowing her son's bright blue eye to immediately capture one's attention.

Stephanie Carpenter, Sandusky, Ohio

Supplies: Patterned paper (Robin's Nest); square brads (Making Memories); navy cardstock; transparency; acrylic paint

Queen for a Day

Since Shannon didn't have a professional photographer for her wedding, she took a variety of photos herself, including this one. To create "patterned paper" accents digitally, she photographed white fabric flowers, traditional patterned papers and ribbon, then changed their hues and resized them all on the computer.

Shannon Freeman, Bellingham, Washington

Supplies: Drawing program (MicroGrafx Draw); Image-editing software (Microsoft Photo Editor); paint program (Microsoft Paint)

Dirty Feet

Barefoot weather and children lead to one inevitable combination...dirty feet! Cynthia celebrated this part of childhood on a simple layout that showcases the "line up" of dirty feet at her house.

Cynthia Coulon, Provo, Utah

Supplies: Patterned papers and leather letters (Rusty Pickle); stickers (EK Success); black stamping ink; brads

A Mother Holds...

There is nothing that tugs at one's heartstrings quite like an infant's hand protectively cradled in her mother's. Melissa melted three different colors of extra thick embossing powder onto a label holder to coordinate with her background papers. She also repurposed a jewelry clasp to dress up her journaling block.

Melissa Kelley, Pueblo, Colorado

Supplies: Patterned paper (Club Scrap); tan and navy cardstocks; label holder; vellum; fibers; clear embossing ink; extra thick embossing powder; brads

About Your Feet

Heidi didn't start scrapbooking until her oldest three children were no longer babies, so when her fourth and last child arrived, she immersed herself in the details of this new little person, including her tiny feet.

Heidi "Deidre" Bishop, Belvidere, Illinois
Photos: Ron Murray, Udderly Graphic, Rockford, Illinois

Supplies: Patterned paper (Daisy D's); metal plaque and eyelet letters (Making Memories); burgundy and green cardstocks; vellum; mulberry paper; fibers; brads

Window to Your Soul

Mary-Catherine's son has intense eyes, a characteristic she echoed with a dramatically enlarged photo, varied textures and saturated colors. She made text into design elements by using rub-ons, letters stamped on copper frames, label tape and patterned paper.

Mary-Catherine Kropinski, Coquitlam, British Columbia, Canada

Supplies: Patterned papers (K & Company, Wordsworth); rub-on letters and embossed metal strip (Making Memories); copper frames (Nunn Design); copper strips (Lee Valley); letter stamps (FontWerks); red cardstock; stamping ink; label tape; date stamp; brads; vellum

Yesterday

Yesterday Tarri's children took baths but today they're taking showers. She encapsulates the bittersweetness of watching children grow with wistful journaling and a photo of her youngest son's bath-wrinkled feet. Tags and a journaling block dyed with walnut ink echo the theme of passing time.

Tarri Botwinski, Grand Rapids, Michigan

Supplies: Patterned papers (Chatterbox, Creative Imaginations, Karen Foster Design, 7 Gypsies); letter stickers (Provo Craft); faux wax seal (Creative Imaginations); brick and cream cardstocks; stamping ink; walnut ink; fibers; tags; eyelets; chalks

Bubbles

A simply sophisticated layout showcases a mother and child exploring the wonder that is a bubble. Koren trimmed around bubbles from patterned paper to subtly frame her photograph.

Koren Jimenez, Houston, Texas

Supplies: Patterned paper (Amscan); printed ribbon (Making Memories); light blue and white cardstocks; vellum

Travels

Photos taken from a different perspective, like this one of a daddy's arms wrapped around his baby son, can make a powerful, emotional statement. Ali added a simple strip of patterned transparency to embellish the layout.

Ali McLaughlin, Bristow, Virginia

Supplies: Patterned paper (7 Gypsies); definition sticker (Making Memories); patterned transparency (K & Company); brick red and tan cardstocks

The Family Ears

Photos from different generations come together in a whimsical layout about a prominent family trait—the ears! Dar created her own unique buckle with two metal rectangles, strips of cardstock, brads and thread to tie them together.

Dar Kaso, Virginia Beach, Virginia

Supplies: Patterned paper (Chatterbox); cardstock letters (Foofala); metal rectangles (7 Gypsies); slate and cream cardstocks; brads; tags; black stamping ink; thread

Precious Shoulders

How crazy to think that these soft, tiny shoulders will someday be part of the broad, strong back of a man—a feeling that Sam captures in a poem used as journaling. She stenciled a harlequin design on patterned paper before printing journaling over it.

Sam Cousins, Trumbull, Connecticut

Supplies: Patterned papers (KI Memories); sticker letters and epoxy stickers (Creative Imaginations); metal square (7 Gypsies); clock face stamps (Make An Impression, Uptown Design Company); black cardstock; clock cut-out; chain; fibers; vellum; transparency; white chalk stamping ink

Blue Eyes

Elsa chose the perfect shades of cardstock and patterned paper to emphasize the color of her son's eyes. She painted and sanded metal embellishments to coordinate and added a piece of blue sea glass for a finishing touch.

Elsa Duff, Whitecourt, Alberta, Canada

Supplies: Patterned papers (Carolee's Creations, Chatterbox); metal words and photo clips (Making Memories); letter tags (Bazzill); wood letters (Li'l Davis Designs); letter snaps (All My Memories); acrylic label holder (KI Memories); sea glass (Magic Scraps); olive and blue cardstocks; acrylic paint; flax; brads

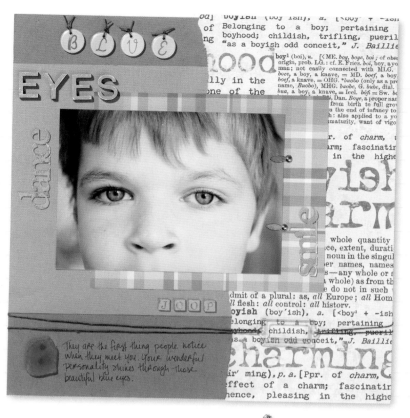

Precious Soles

Sam jumped on a moment when her kids were all lined up in bed to take this darling photo of the most precious soles in her life. She added the title to the photo with image-editing software before she had it printed so when her prints came back, the title was already done and ready to go!

Sam Cousins, Trumbull, Connecticut

Supplies: Patterned papers and vellum (EK Success); label sticker (Pebbles); image-editing software (Adobe Photoshop); buttons; fibers; black stamping ink

Hands

Jessica raided her local hardware store for many elements on this page, including the twine, hinges, stencils and sandpaper for distressing the edges of her photo. She accented stencils with stamping ink and bits of twine for an eye-catching title.

Jessica Bellus, Minot Air Force Base, North Dakota

Supplies: Patterned paper (Chatterbox); black and rust cardstocks; letter stencils; twine; hinges; brads

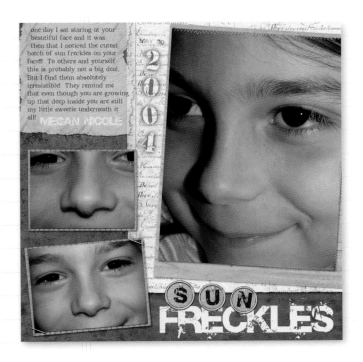

Sun Freckles

Amy was admiring her daughter's face one day and thought her tiny freckles deserved a page in her scrapbook. She used a combination of digitally created "papers" and traditional papers that she purchased and scanned.

Amy Edwards, Newark Valley, New York

Supplies: Image-editing software (Adobe Photoshop); pink and brown papers and tags (Jennifer Ditterich); script patterned paper (7 Gypsies); vellum (www.scrapbook-elements.com); stencil numbers (www.gauchogirl.com); digital elements (www.scrapbook-bytes.com)

Sunshine on Your Shoulders

There are few things that make Matthew happier than spending time in the sun and the water, which leads to a great tan on his shoulders! Shannon stamped and embossed title letters then connected them together with coordinating string.

Shannon Montez, San Jose, California

Supplies: Patterned paper (Amscan); letter stickers (Creative Imaginations); letter stamps (Hero Arts); brown, tan and cream cardstocks; chalk; string; tags; jump ring

B is for Birthday

birth•day (berth -dá) n. the day of a person's birth, or a thing's beginning

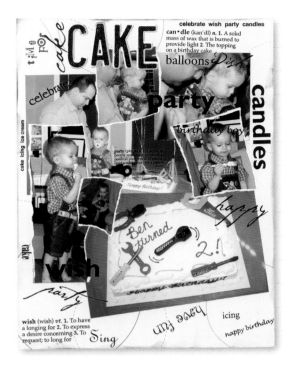

Time for Cake

Sam had a collection of not-so-great photos from her son's birthday, so she tore them apart and collaged them together to make a great layout. A few definitions, words and letter stickers add finishing touches.

Sam Cousins, Trumbull, Connecticut

Supplies: Patterned paper (KI Memories); rub-on words (AC Moore); letter stickers (Sticker Studio); letter stamps (PSX Design); black stamping ink

Happy Birthday

A fresh take on cropping photos draws attention to the pictures on this layout. and leads the viewer's eye right into the heart of the layout. Birthday party hats perk up a celebratory title by standing in for the letter A.

Bonnie Gokey, Sugar Hill, Georgia

Supplies: Border photo and letter stickers (EK Success); printed transparency (Magic Scraps); yellow, red and blue cardstocks; slide mount

All Girl

A darling girl smiling in front of a birthday cupcake is the perfect focal point for this fun, all-girl page. Christine attached pink and black ribbons to the end of a label-maker-style sticker for embellishment at the top of the page.

Christine Traversa, Joliet, Illinois

Supplies: Patterned paper (Wordsworth); stickers (Creative Imaginations, Pebbles); clear pocket (EK Success); date stamp (Making Memories); black and white cardstocks; black stamping ink; ribbon; eyelets; fibers

It's My Party...

Angela says her daughter cries at the drop of a hat, so she wasn't surprised when Ashlyn burst into tears in front of her birthday cake. Of course, Mom had to snap a couple of quick photos before running to comfort her daughter!

Angela Mihalow, Minneapolis, Minnesota

Supplies: Patterned paper (Chatterbox); metal word and letter (Making Memories); letter stickers (EK Success, Me & My Big Ideas, Sandylion); letter stamps (PSX Design); tag die cut (Quic-Kutz); eyelet; black stamping ink; sewing machine; safety pin

First Celebration

White acrylic paint dry-brushed across blue cardstock adds interest to this lively 1-year-old's birthday page. Stacy gave round metal letter tags a makeover by cutting off the sides. Two rectangular metal-rimmed tags serve as frames for cropped photos.

Stacy Yoder, Yucaipa, California

Supplies: Metal letter tags, rub-on letters, metal-rimmed tags, metal word (Making Memories); candle die cut (EK Success); red, white and blue cardstocks; string; buttons; brads; corrugated paper

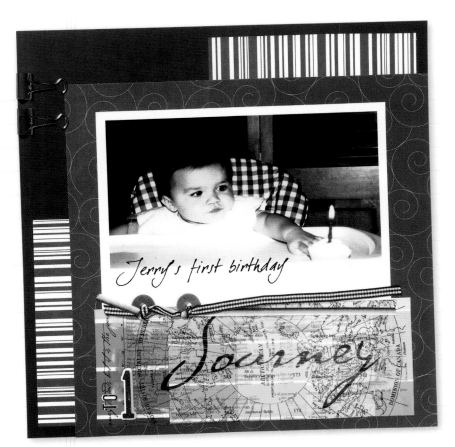

Jerry's First Birthday

Paint chips and acrylic paint behind a patterned transparency add a splash of bright color to this black-and-white page. Little Jerry's wary expression adds a bit of drama as well.

Peggy Manrique, Manchester Center, Vermont

Supplies: Patterned papers (Chatterbox, KI Memories); patterned transparency (Creative Imaginations); word washers (Making Memories); sticker letters (Sticker Studio); black cardstock; ribbon; acrylic paint; silver binder clips; paint chips

Backyard Birthday

Cherie wanted to include her daughter's birthday cards on a page without making them the focus, so she enlarged and matted one photo, then sewed three edges to the background to create a card pocket. She outlined her title with black pen to pop against the pink background.

Cherie Ward, Colorado Springs, Colorado

Supplies: Patterned papers (Daisy D's, EK Success, K & Company); foam letter stamps (Making Memories); butterfly stamps (Close To My Heart); label tag (Chatterbox); rub-on letters (Creative Imaginations); light pink, medium pink, purple and white cardstocks; black and watermark stamping inks; chalk; glitter glue; ribbon; acrylic paint; transparency; foam tape

Happy Birthday Two You

Memories of young Alyssa's 2nd birthday were recorded on a folded tag tucked safely inside a decorated pink envelope. Amy converted the photos to black and white, but preserved the colors of her daughter's cake in her paper choices.

Amy Howe, Frisco, Texas

Supplies: Patterned papers (SEI); definition paper (KI Memories); letter stickers (Bo-Bunny Press, Making Memories); accordion tag (DMD); label tape (Dymo); license plate tiles and alphabet button (Junkitz); envelope (Designer's Library); black and white cardstocks; black stamping ink; ribbon; paper clip, silk flowers; circle tag; brads; jump ring

Let There Be Cake

Amy captured her daughter's uncertainty about her first birthday cake in this photo. Colorful fabric scraps adhered with a few well-placed staples make up her photo mat.

Amy Howe, Frisco, Texas

Supplies: Frame die cut and acrylic candle (KI Memories); stencil (Autumn Leaves); fabric (Junkitz); pink, green and white cardstocks; staples; transparency; black stamping ink

The Cake

Journaling tucked under a hinged photo explains about the "smash cake," an important 1-year-old tradition in Cherie's family. When a spot on her focal-point photo was accidentally scratched, Cherie sanded all the edges to blend it in.

Cherie Ward, Colorado Springs, Colorado

Supplies: Patterned papers (Chatterbox, K & Company, KI Memories, Mustard Moon); letter stamps (Ma Vinci's Reliquary); flower stamp (Delta); embossed metal border, hinges, and woven label (Making Memories); olive, lime, dark pink, pink and white cardstocks; stamping ink; watermark ink; glitter glue; acrylic paint; jewels; thread; transparency; twill tape

Anna's 1st Birthday

Circles create a playful rhythm across this birthday spread. Cherie scanned photos from a Chuck E. Cheese party then reduced and printed them in black-and-white, creating an artful contrast to the strong colors of the spread.

Cherie Ward, Colorado Springs, Colorado

Supplies: Patterned papers and large letter stickers (Doodlebug Design); small letter stickers (KI Memories); dark red, red, pink and white cardstocks; vellum

Birthday in Blue

That moment in a 2-year-old's life when she realizes that all eyes are on her as the birthday girl can be overwhelming, as is sweetly captured on this textured page. Ashley painted a piece of torn corrugated cardboard for a unique photo mat. Cheesecloth peeps through a handcut number 2 on a square tag.

Ashley Calder, Dundas, Ontario, Canada

Supplies: Patterned papers (Chatterbox); corner accent (Nunn Design); shaped clip (7 Gypsies); slate blue, ocean, and light blue cardstocks; corrugated cardboard; acrylic paint; ribbon; clip; snowflake charm; blue stamping ink; silk flower; cheesecloth

Birthdays Bring Joy

Mary loved the bright colors in her daughter's dress and hair ribbon so she incorporated them into her layout. A hidden tag holds the story of her daughter's two big gifts: a two-wheeled bicycle and her very first ring.

Mary Healea, Fairborn, Ohio

Supplies: Letter stickers (Creative Imaginations, Karen Foster Design, Me & My Big Ideas); flower die cut (Colorbök); letter stamps (Ma Vinci's Reliquary, PSX Design); label holder and flower brad (Making Memories); label tape (Dymo); lime, orange and white cardstocks; ribbon; brads; black, pink, orange and green stamping inks; safety pin; flower charm

C is for Couples

couple (kup´ el) n. anything joining two things together; bond; link

Chris and Chacy

Amy's beautifully collaged layout is the perfect setting for a romantic wedding photo. Amy intertwined the letter stickers in her title to look like the new couple's monogram.

Amy Stultz, Mooresville, Indiana

Supplies: Patterned paper and phrase stickers (Pebbles); textured cardstock and printed transparency (Memories Complete); letter stickers (K & Company); deco brads and date stamp (Making Memories); flower die cuts (Leeco); stamping ink; acrylic paint; photo corners

You Color My World

Two mirror-image photos, one black-and-white and one in color, graphically illustrate this husband's assertion that life was gray before he met his wife. Patricia printed color bars directly on the vellum along with her title and journaling.

Patricia Anderson, Selah, Washington

Supplies: Black, red and white cardstocks; vellum; brads; sewing machine

Love

Amy was so inspired by her sister's loving marriage, she created a page as a tribute to them. She sanded a collection of tiny tag stickers and threaded them together for a fresh, fun border.

Amy Howe, Frisco, Texas

Supplies: Patterned paper and tag stickers (Pebbles); letter stickers (Paper Loft); title sticker (Creative Imaginations); printed ribbon (Making Memories); black and pink cardstocks; staples; brown stamping ink; foam tape

Make a Wish...

Martha felt that these photos were quintessential reflections of young love, so she created this page as a gift for a close friend. Black tulle adds softness and an air of refinement, while a beautiful focal-point photo adds dramatic serenity to this dreamy layout.

Martha Crowther, Salem, New Hampshire

Supplies: Pink and black cardstocks; slide mounts (Magic Scraps); wire; beads; rhinestones; heart charm; tulle; transparency

Worth the Wait

There's an old saying that a single woman over 35 is more likely to be hit by lightning than get married. Not true for Barb. On this layout, she journals about meeting her husband at the end of her thirties and how it was worth the wait.

Barb Hogan, Cincinnati, Ohio

Supplies: Printed transparency (K & Company); letter stamps (PSX Design); ribbon charm (Making Memories); charcoal and white cardstocks; vellum; ribbon; brads

Always

Shelby wove patterned papers, ribbon and rickrack together for a loving appreciation page dedicated to her parents. A woven label with a phrase printed on it serves as her title.

Shelby Valadez, Saugus, California

Supplies: Patterned papers (Chatterbox); printed ribbon and woven label (Making Memories); blue cardstock; tag; rickrack; walnut ink; brown stamping ink

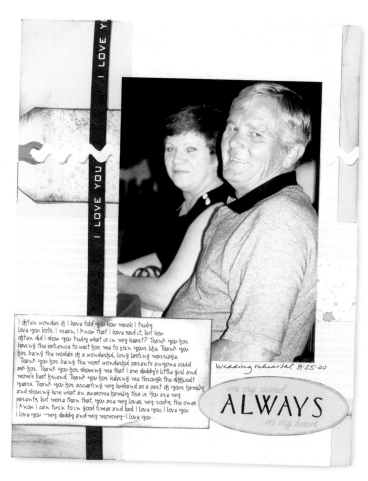

Blessed By You

Inspired by a Pottery Barn advertisement, Susan used strips of patterned paper to break this page into sections. A collection of hearts in similar styles lines the bottom to support the page theme.

Susan Wyno, Puyallup, Washington
Photo: Alex Tinsman, Renton, Washington

Supplies: Patterned papers (7 Gypsies, Chatterbox); heart sticker (Westrim); mesh eyelets, heart clip and metal heart (Making Memories); photo corners (Kolo); cocoa and rust cardstocks; ribbon; brads; charm; ribbon flower

Us

Janice and her husband discovered that once their child was born they had hardly any time for each other, so she created this layout as a reminder of the special times they spent camping together. She created the background of this layout on the computer. Since her photos were not the best quality, she textured them and made them translucent to mask their imperfections.

Janice Dye-Szucs, Oshawa, Ontario, Canada

Supplies: Image-editing software (Adobe Photoshop); background (www.scrapbookgraphics.com)

Love

Rebecca created this layout when her 12-year marriage hit a rough spot to remind herself of how she felt when she married her husband. She covered a basic photo mat board with patterned paper and sanded the edges for a soft look.

Rebecca Chabot, Sanford, Maine

Supplies: Patterned paper (Sweetwater); fleur de lis punch (McGill); heart punch (Emagination Crafts); envelope template (Green Sneakers); sage, burgundy and tan cardstocks; hemp cord; crochet thread; watermark ink; photo mat; scalloped scissors; acrylic paint; thread

Love

Think back to when your grandparents were young and imagine them in the throes of early love. This photo evokes that time for Melissa, who finds comfort in the fact that different generations are not so different after all.

Melissa Kelley, Pueblo, Colorado

Supplies: Patterned papers (Scenic Route Paper Co.); stickers (Pebbles); twill tape (Wright's); ribbon (May Arts, Offray); black cardstock; black stamping ink; transparency

My Parents

Martha celebrated her parents' 40th anniversary with a then-and-now page. She included a small tag booklet full of fun facts about her parents, including their ages when they married, schools they attended, their honeymoon destination and where they purchased their first home.

Martha Crowther, Salem, New Hampshire

Supplies: Patterned papers (Autumn Leaves); frame (Daisy D's); slide mount (Creative Imaginations); foam stamp (Making Memories); love sticker (NRN Designs); cream cardstock; ribbon; fibers; chalk; acrylic paint

Together

Karen told her nephew's love story through photos rather than words. This young couple has known each other every moment of their lives and is now engaged. She layered a patterned transparency and rose cut-out over orange cardstock, then tied ribbons through eyelets at the bottom of the transparency.

Karen Buck, West Chester, Ohio

Supplies: Patterned papers (7 Gypsies, Paperwhite); printed transparency (Creative Imaginations); metal plate (K & Company); orange and rust cardstocks; ribbon; eyelets

C is for Culture

culture (kul´cher) n. development, improvement, or refinement of the intellect, emotions, interests, manners or taste

I never studied Native American history until I was pregnant with my son Cooper. Half his blood is Western Band Cherokee and I felt it to be top priority to teach my son about his heritage the best I could since he had no living representatives in his life.

The more history I learned the more I felt it important to educate others about our lands first citizens and celebrate their heritage. I pride myself in addressing the educational issue with my sons teachers, school system & with the general public. I dream that one day, to have compiled Native stories, poems and quotes for children to read about in their school libraries.

"I wish it to be remembered that I was the last man of my tribe to surrender my rifle." - Sitting Bull, Hunkpapa Sioux leader surrendering, July 19, 1881

Discover the Beauty

Carla felt it was important to record her educational journey into her son's Western Band Cherokee roots as part of her "All About Me" scrapbook project. She downloaded Native American images from the Internet, printed them on vellum and painted them with decoupage glue.

Carla Jacobsen, Lebanon, Tennessee

Supplies: Patterned paper (K & Company); Native American images and mosaic tiles (www.alteredpages.com); sticker (PSX Design); rub-on words (Making Memories); letter stamps (Hero Arts); metallic rub-ons (Craf-T); postage stamps; chalk; vellum; decoupage glue

Kintai

Samantha choose mesh paper as a page background to mimic the idea of a fish net. Decorated bits of "sea china"—natural elements with smooth edges that wash ashore in Japan— were used as photo corners and as accents above her journaling.

Samantha Walker, Battle Ground, Washington

Supplies: Mesh paper and paper bark strip (FLAX art & design); metal label holder (Jo-Ann Fabrics); watercolor paper; tan cardstock; turquoise and tan vellums; embossing powder; brads; brown stamping ink; sea china; sewing machine

The Kintai river had a mystical setting the night we went to visit. The sun was setting. There was a low fog on the river, and the Kamarat fishing boats were lined up in a row at the docks waiting for the festivities of the night; when their lanterns would be lit to lure the fish below into the trap of the fisherman's bird companions. This age old Japanese tradition still exists today but rather as a ceremonial event than a way of life. I am always intrigued by the traditions of another culture.

1997

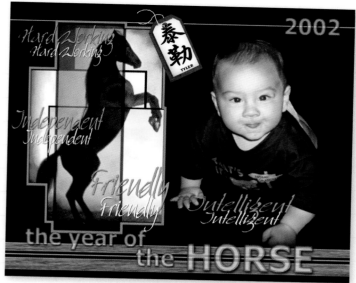

The Year of the Horse/
The Year of the Dragon

One of the ways Rachel celebrates her sons' heritage is by making them Chinese zodiac pages. Digitally made tags display her sons' names written in Chinese characters.

Rachel Dickson, Calgary, Alberta, Canada

Supplies: Image-editing software (Adobe Photoshop, Microsoft Digital Image Pro)

Pollera

Jen was so struck by the brightly colored pollera so common in Panama, she gave them their own page in her scrapbook. She invoked the spirit of these traditional brightly colored dresses with her background paper, strips of fabric and architecture-style embellishments that she painted.

Jen Lowe, Lafayette, Colorado

Supplies: Patterned paper (Reminiscence Papers); architecture-style embellishments (EK Success); rub-on words (Making Memories); turquoise and white cardstocks; acrylic paints; clear embossing ink; clear embossing powder; cut-out illustration; fabric

All the Queen's Horses

On this page of English culture, Trudy reminisces that she felt a rumbling in the ground that echoed through her bones as hundreds and hundreds of the Queen's soldiers came into view during the Golden Jubilee parade. Her panoramic photo communicates the scale and grandeur of the occasion, as well as her pride in being a British subject.

Trudy Sigurdson, Victoria, British Columbia, Canada

Supplies: Patterned paper (7 Gypsies); black trim (Me & My Big Ideas); scrapbook nails (Chatterbox); black and cream cardstocks; black stamping ink; foam tape

To Aspire

Arlene digitally merged photos of a presentation from the Halau (hula school) into a stunning design that shows the "elite" dancers looking down on the keiki (children) who aspire to be like them. She incorporated the Hawaiian word meaning "to teach or to educate" into her background and changed the tint of her photos to represent the different groups of dancers.

Arlene Santos, Mililani, Hawaii

Supplies: Image-editing software (Adobe Photoshop)

Crossing Dance

This spread celebrates the African rite of passage called the Crossing Dance. Maria kept her embellishments minimal so the focus remains on her photos and the detailed story she recounts in her journaling.

Maria Newport, Smyrna, Georgia

Supplies: Patterned papers (Colors by Design, Making Memories); metal letters (Making Memories); mint cardstock; eyelets; fibers

When In... Do As...

Touches of Asian and European cultures come together in this lively travel page. Wire woven through the edges of photo mats provide an interesting touch while Chinese and Spanish keys add international flair.

Tricia Rubens, Castle Rock, Colorado

Supplies: Patterned papers and journal pages (Rusty Pickle); rub-on letters (Provo Craft); printed twill (7 Gypsies); key (Magic Scraps); Chinese key (Boxer Scrapbook Productions); decorative brads (Creative Impressions); rubber stamps (Inkadinkado); brown stamping ink; tags; walnut ink; fibers; wire; mesh; embroidery floss; ribbon

Dancing

Velvet fabrics, netting, ribbon and beads mimic the textures of the dancer's costume in this exotic page about a Moroccan belly dancer at the Epcot Center. Pam applied metallic rub-ons to the cardstock background to give it a subtle shimmer and added beads and glitter to double-stick tape to create eye-catching photo mats.

Pam Canavan, Clermont, Florida

Supplies: Tinsel, glitter and mosaic tiles (Magic Scraps); hanging bead trim (Hirschberg Schutz & Co.); beads (Little Black Dress Designs); definition sticker and metal corners (Making Memories); letter stickers (Creative Imaginations); small spiral clips (7 Gypsies); circle clips (Target); metallic rub-ons (Craf-T); brown cardstock; fabric; velvet; tulle; vellum

D is for Dirt

dirt (dûrt) n. any unclean or soiling matter

3rd Birthday Present

Sand-colored cardstock makes a natural backdrop for a set of sand-covered toes. Patterned paper cut into strips is a simple yet effective embellishment on a page about a birthday girl enjoying her new sandbox.

Peggy Manrique, Manchester Center, Vermont

Supplies: Patterned paper (7 Gypsies, Chatterbox); letter stickers (Sticker Studio); rub-on words (Making Memories); brown cardstock; ribbon

Diggin' Dirt

Stamping ink around the edges gives each element on this page its own muddy look. Melodee discovered that a belt loop from an old pair of jeans made the perfect tab for her journaling tag and a toy truck rolled across an ink pad looks quite like mud-caked tire tracks.

Melodee Langworthy, Rockford, Michigan

Supplies: Patterned paper and stickers (Karen Foster Design); stencils (Ma Vinci's Reliquary); decorative eyelets (Creative Imaginations); cream and brown cardstocks; tag; stamping ink; denim belt loop

stinky dirty BOYS

The **boy's will** is the wind's will, and the thoughts of youth are **long, long thoughts.**

Jacob and Matthew need only a warm day and water and they are in heaven! They played outside on the unusually warm March afternoon of 2004, and got so dirty I told them they needed to be hosed down. Well, they took me literally!

FUN wild & crazy

Stinky Dirty Boys

Little did Heather know that when she told her boys that they were so dirty they should be hosed down, they would take her literally! Clean, graphic lines offer an artful counterpoint to the dirty, wrinkled toes and sloppy, wet-haired grins in her photos.

Heather Uppencamp, Provo, Utah

Supplies: Patterned paper (Mustard Moon); woven labels (Making Memories); black and sage cardstocks; transparency

d.

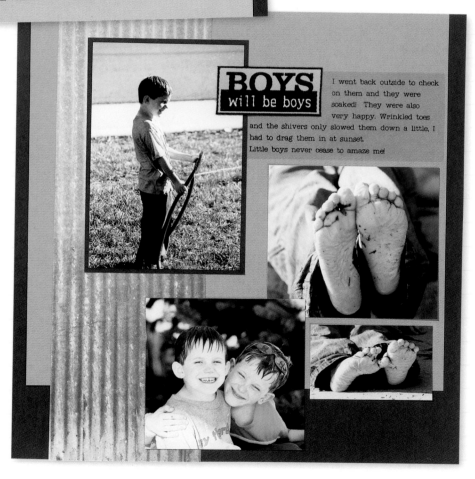

BOYS will be boys

I went back outside to check on them and they were soaked! They were also very happy. Wrinkled toes and the shivers only slowed them down a little, I had to drag them in at sunset. Little boys never cease to amaze me!

So Much to Do

Mow the yard, shovel, water, mow, water, rake, shovel, water...whew! Laura tucked her young son's fake "to-do" list underneath her focal-point photo along with photo evidence featuring Griffin's skills of wielding a lawn mower and shovel.

Laura McKinley, Westport, Connecticut

Supplies: Patterned paper (Chatterbox, Making Memories, 7 Gypsies); letter stickers (Creative Imaginations, Li'l Davis Designs, Paper Loft, Pebbles, Rusty Pickle); twill tape (7 Gypsies); file folder and decorative paper clip (EK Success); khaki and black cardstocks; ribbon; eyelets; jump rings; brown pen

Mud Bud Club

One to man the hose, two to throw mud at each other and another to be ready with mud pack hair treatments... the Mud Buds! Busy background paper, torn and inked journaling and messy fibers give you a peek into the chaos these culprits created one summer afternoon.

Martha Crowther, Salem, New Hampshire

Supplies: Patterned papers (Karen Foster Design, Paper Loft); stickers (Paper Loft); red, gray and rust cardstocks; slide frame (Design Originals); plaque (DieCuts with a View); overall buckles; fibers; hemp cord; brown stamping ink; negative film strip

Yourself

Yum...rocks! This little guy's serious face takes center stage as Christy's journaling hides beneath a fitting quote. A rub-on title completes the simple look.

Christy Spruiell, Darmstadt, Germany

Supplies: Patterned paper and quote (Karen Foster Design); rub-on word, hinge, photo flips and washer (Making Memories); teal and white cardstocks; fibers; snaps; chalk; brown stamping ink

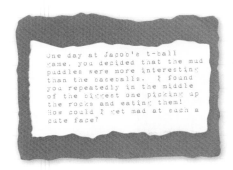

Play in the Mud

Nicola was ironing her son's shorts one day when she came across a tiny bit of hidden treasure—a pebble in his pocket. She included the pebble as a page embellishment along with premade accents.

Nicola Clarke, Basildon, Essex, United Kingdom

Supplies: Patterned paper (Making Memories, Sweetwater); printed fabric (Creative Imaginations); printed transparencies (Daisy D's, K & Company); printed vellum and t-pin (EK Success); word stickers (Creative Imaginations, Making Memories, Me & My Big Ideas, Pebbles); file folder (Autumn Leaves); canvas phrase (Li'l Davis Designs); circle die cuts (KI Memories); tan, brown and black cardstocks; fabric; staples; thread; extra thick embossing enamel; vintage image; negative film; pebbles

Built Tough

During an outing to the park, Cyndi's husband threatened to tape record all the things she said to her son as he wallowed in the dirt. Instead, Cyndi captured these messy incidents on a layout. She stamped phrases on tan cardstock blocks then painted them with walnut ink before the stamping was completely dry for a smeared, dirty look.

Cyndi Habib, Gilbert, Arizona

Supplies: Color blocking template (Deluxe Designs); letter stamps (Hero Arts); woven labels (Making Memories); letter stickers (Creative Imaginations); label holder (Hirschberg Schutz & Co.); java, tan, kraft, blue and red cardstocks; clear lacquer; dirt; brown and black stamping inks; brads; walnut ink

Mud

Is it Petie, the dog from "The Little Rascals," or Dana's daughter Carlie? You decide! Dana dipped her fingers in brown acrylic paint for extra "muddy" touches on this page.

Dana Swords, Doswell, Virginia

Supplies: Patterned paper (Karen Foster Design); black, brown, tan and turquoise cardstocks; acrylic paint; brown stamping ink

D is for Dream

dream (drem) n. a fanciful vision of the conscious mind;
daydream; fantasy; reverie

While we were waiting for Miss Pat to
come back so that we could say
goodbye, I caught Jonathan
daydreaming and holding his hand like
Spiderman does when he is shooting a
web. It just shows how obsessed he
really is with Spiderman, that he
unknowingly holds his hand that way.
~Class Easter Party 2004

Dreaming of Spiderman

Jeannie knew her son was obsessed with Spiderman when
she caught him daydreaming and unconsciously holding
his hand the way Spiderman does when spinning his web.
She highlighted this characteristic hand gesture with a
watch crystal. Swipes of acrylic paint decorate the bottom
of the page.

Jeannie van Wert, Tampa, Florida

Supplies: Patterned paper (Carolee's Creations); hinges (Making
Memories); stencil letter (Ma Vinci's Reliquary); letter stamps (Hero
Arts, Making Memories, Postmodern Design); black and tan cardstocks; handmade paper; mesh; brads; twill tape; watch crystal;
embossing powder; gold leafing pen; acrylic paint

As I tiptoe into your bedroom each night
to pull up the covers and tuck you in tight,
I linger longer just watching you sleep,
and think of our day and the memories I'll keep.

My sweet, sweet Brendan,
You have no idea how much I love this time of the night.
During the day you go non-stop without ever taking a break.
You are so busy all day long...playing, watching TV, coloring,
drawing and then playing some more. Your imagination is so
active all day long. And you are so inquisitive...you have to
know the answers to everything! Some times you just wear
me out! That's why I love these few minutes at night when
you're asleep and I can just watch you **DREAM** quietly.
I love you.
mommy
xoxo

Dream

This page showcases a mom's love for the time of
night when her ever-moving son finally slows down.
Soft, pastel colors set a peaceful, dreamy stage for
photos of a sleeping boy.

Dee Gallimore-Perry, Griswold, Connecticut

Supplies: Patterned papers and circle tag inserts (KI Memories); die-cut frame (My Mind's Eye); letter stickers (Chatterbox, Creative Imaginations); dog tag (Chronicle Books);
star charms, hinges, and rub-on word (Making Memories);
alphabet stamps (PSX Design); metal-rimmed tags; ribbon;
black stamping ink; thread; date stamp

Dream

A tender photo of a small child ready for sleep is the perfect accompaniment for a mother's thoughtful musings about dreams. This clean, straightforward page keeps the attention on Amy's daughter's face.

Amy Goldstein, Kent Lakes, New York

Supplies: Patterned papers (7 Gypsies); charms (www.ScrapsAhoy.com); pink and rose card-stocks; ribbon; circle clip; brads

as you lay SLEEPING my heart aches at the beauty of your face.
the gentle FLUTTER of your eyes. rosebud lips purse and pucker. an ANGEL'S KISS perhaps?
a tender sigh, a TINY half smile
what are you DREAMIN my little one?
sunny days and butterflies.
a MAGICAL unicorn
that flies an angel's visit from HEAVEN above?
a brand new teddybear to LOVE?
well dream away my sweet BABY
and may all your DREAMS come to be.

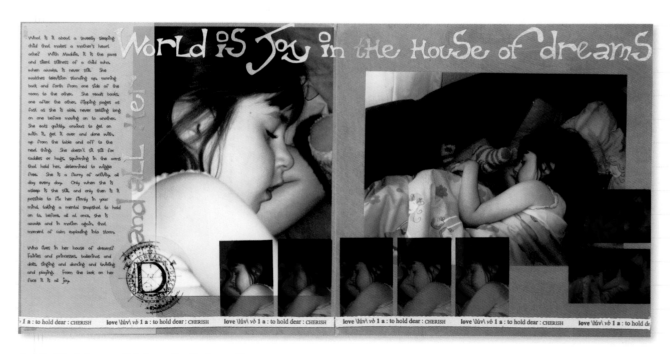

And All Her World Is Joy

Changing photos to black-and-white gives them a classic, dreamy quality that is perfect for the treasured image of a sleeping child. Mary Anne used image-editing software to make one photo purple, then printed it on a transparency for an eye-catching embellishment.

Mary Anne Walters, Ramsdell, Hampshire, United Kingdom

Supplies: Patterned papers (Creative Imaginations); printed twill tape (7 Gypsies); downloaded "D" image; vellum; transparency

'Godspeed (Sweet Dreams)'
Dixie Chicks

Dragon tales and the "water is wide"
Pirate's sail and lost boys fly
Fish bite moonbeams every night
And I love you

Godspeed, little man
Sweet dreams, little man
Oh my love will fly to you each night on angels wings
Godspeed
Sweet dreams

The rocket racer's all tuckered out
Superman's in pajamas on the couch
Goodnight moon, we'll find the mouse
And I love you

Godspeed, little man
Sweet dreams, little man
Oh my love will fly to you each night on angels wings
Godspeed
Sweet dreams

God bless mommy and match box cars
God bless dad and thanks for the stars
God heard "Amen," wherever you are
And I love you

Godspeed, little man
Sweet dreams, little man
Oh my love will fly to you each night on angels wings
Godspeed
Godspeed
Godspeed
Sweet dreams

January 18, 2004

Godspeed, Sweet Dreams

What parent has not had the heartbreaking experience of listening to a child wail in protest at any suggestion of taking The Dreaded Nap? When Jennifer found her son curled up on her rocking chair, finally sound asleep, she created this layout with some Dixie Chicks lyrics to remind herself that the exhausted child will eventually sleep.

Jennifer Massaro, South Plainfield, New Jersey

Supplies: Patterned paper (Chatterbox); letter stamps (Ma Vinci's Reliquary); blue cardstock; blue stamping ink

My Dreams for You

This pensive photograph presented a wonderful opportunity for Jodi to scrapbook some of the hopes and dreams she has for her daughter. Thin strips of patterned paper tied into knots embellish her title tags, the corners of her photo mat and layout.

Jodi Amidei, Memory Makers Books

Supplies: Patterned papers (Diane's Daughters); letter tiles (Li'l Davis Designs); slate, cream, tan and navy cardstocks; brown stamping ink; foam tape

Dream a Little Dream for Me

A dramatic enlargement of one little whirlwind's rare moment of repose forms the centerpiece of this simple page. Michelle stamped the main word of her title then printed the rest on a transparency and overlaid the stamped word.

Michelle Tornay, Newark, California

Supplies: Patterned paper, border strip and tag (Chatterbox); letter stamps (Making Memories); sand and blue cardstocks; brads; acrylic paint; brown stamping ink; transparency

d

Sweet Dream

An art piece found online with strong geometric shapes inspired Monica's page design. She layered premade and handcut circles with patterned paper to give the page a strong sense of shape.

Monica Anderson, Glendale, Arizona

Supplies: Patterned paper (Daisy D's); printed tags (Pebbles); definition sticker (Making Memories); epoxy word stickers (Creative Imaginations); khaki and dark brown cardstocks; brown stamping ink

When You Wake

Morning light from a bedroom window shining across a sleeping child's face creates a great photo opportunity. A fabric pocket holds Wendy's wistful words about stopping time in the light of a new morning.

Wendy Malichio, Bethel, Connecticut

Supplies: Patterned paper (Mustard Moon); textured paper (Jennifer Collection); dimensional clock sticker (K & Company); fabric pocket (Li'l Davis Designs); letter stickers (Creative Imaginations); clock stamp (Art Impressions); printed vellum (NRN Designs); black stamping ink; transparency

Sleep my sweet boy, for when you wake yet another moment will have come and gone. Sometimes I feel things are so rushed in our lives and I wish I could just freeze time. I know that one day will come, much too soon, and you will be a young man. I will no longer have my little boy tugging at my leg, asking me to play super heroes. I love that moment in the morning, right before I wake you. The sun is shining on your sweet face, and you look so peaceful. I really do treasure these quiet "almost frozen in time" moments. (2004)
Love, Mom

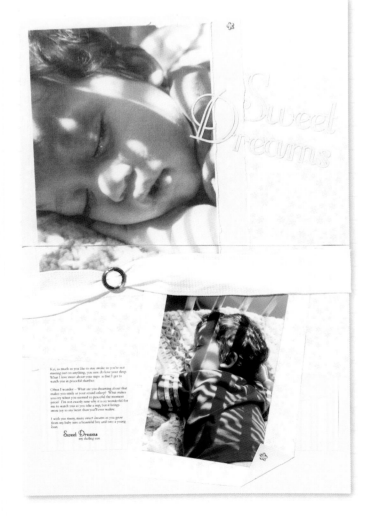

Sweet Dreams

Sherry turned 8½ x 11" pages on their sides for this dreamy layout. She converted her main photo to black-and-white, printed it on cream cardstock, then tore the edges.

Sherry Cartwright, Kempner, Texas

Supplies: Patterned paper (Chatterbox); title laser cut (Sarah Heidt Photocraft); ribbon charm (A Charming Place); flower brads (Making Memories); lemon and cream cardstocks; ribbon

E is for Exercise

exercise (ek´ser siz´) n. activity for the purpose of training or developing the body or mind

Your Hockey Career

His father is convinced he will sign a multimillion dollar contract by the time he's 19, and his mother wants him to go to Harvard before landing in the NHL. Mary captures her budding hockey player's enthusiastic spirit while poking fun at her and her husband's wild parental expectations.

Mary-Catherine Kropinski
Coquitlam, British Columbia, Canada

Supplies: Patterned paper and letter stickers (Paper Loft); sticker (Memories Complete); photo corners (Canson); red cardstock; black stamping ink

Soccer

A full-page preprinted transparency makes a big impression with a small amount of effort. Pam changed her photo to black-and-white, then spot-colored her daughter's jersey for additional impact.

Pam Sivage, Georgetown, Texas

Supplies: Patterned paper (SEI); preprinted transparency (Karen Foster Design); number stickers (Creative Imaginations)

Dance

A simply elegant page is the perfect display for these classic black-and-white photos of a pretty girl in a flowing dress. Jlyne stitched pink maruyama paper to the bottom half of her background for texture and a color boost.

Jlyne Hanback, Biloxi, Mississippi

Supplies: Lavender cardstock; maruyama paper; circle clip; fibers; transparency; thread

Irvine Winter Classic

Debi kept these pages very simple to showcase these amazing action shots of her son in his first soccer tournament. The team placed third, and she scanned and printed a copy of the medal the they received to serve as the page's title.

Debi Boler, Newport Beach, California

Supplies: Patterned paper (Close To My Heart); gray and blue cardstocks; ribbon; foam tape

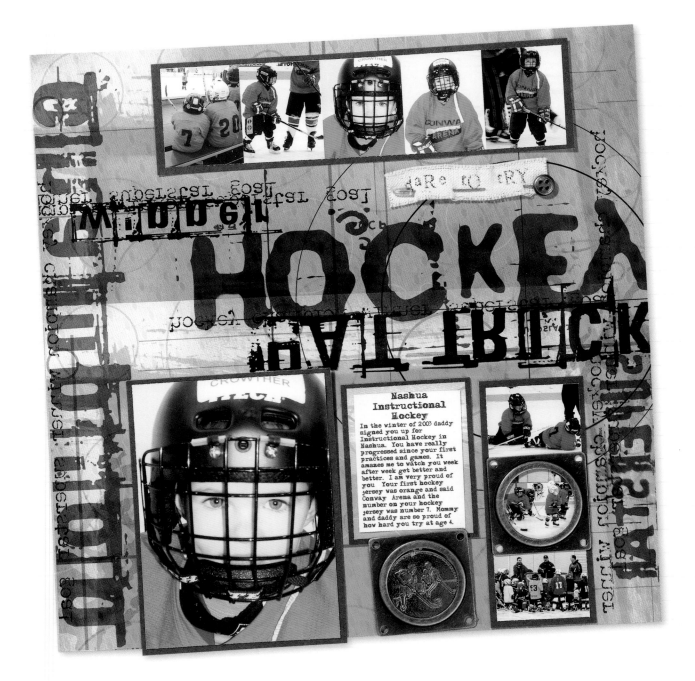

Nashua Instructional Hockey

This layout of her 4-year-old's first hockey game was particularly meaningful for Martha since her husband played semi-professional hockey and her 14-year-old son is an accomplished goalie. A hockey medallion framed in a brass plate feels right at home on this page about the Crowther family's latest up-and-comer.

Martha Crowther, Salem, New Hampshire

Supplies: Patterned papers (Karen Foster Design); patterned transparency (Daisy D's); metal pin (EK Success); brass plates (Li'l Davis Designs); dark gray cardstock; hockey medallion; preprinted canvas

Junior Rookie

Eager anticipation and the love of the game are written all over this little slugger's face. Kerry wanted to give her page the feel of old-time baseball photos, so she changed her photo to sepia and used distressed-looking elements as accents.

Kerry Zerff, Regina, Saskatchewan, Canada

Supplies: Patterned paper, tag and letter stickers (Paper Loft); rub-on letters (Making Memories); stickers and printed transparency (Memories Complete); picture hangers (Scrappin' Extras); snaps; ribbon; black stamping ink

Strut

After his first home run, Ronnie thought it looked like her son strutted off the field, so that became the title of her computer-generated layout. In the open space on the photograph, she added the title and digital baseball lacing.

Ronnie McCray, St. James, Missouri

Supplies: Image-editing software (Adobe Photoshop Elements); baseball lacing (www.scrapbook-bytes.com)

Dugout Time

A lineup of tired T-ball tots made the perfect shot for the last page of a T-ball album. Ronnie created textured papers, a label holder and baseball accent digitally.

Ronnie McCray, St. James, Missouri

Supplies: Image-editing software (Adobe Photoshop Elements)

Born 2 Ride

Luke can ride 12 to 35 miles with his brother and father and still want to ride his bike after he gets home. Michelle dialed up the texture on this rugged layout by using modeling paste on corrugated paper, tiny beads embedded in clear lacquer over painted tin, hemp cord and actual screw heads.

Michelle Pendleton, Colorado Springs, Colorado

Supplies: Patterned paper (Amscan); lettering template (EK Success); square clip, leaf eyelets, word washer, tin square and rectangle tag (Making Memories); modeling paste (Liquitex); tan and sage cardstocks; embossing powder; corrugated cardstock; ribbon; hemp cord; floss; chalk; brown stamping ink; acrylic paint; square punch; embossing ink; clear lacquer; tiny glass marbles; screw heads

Lord of the Rings

Barb's layout pays tribute to her son's favorite part of the playground—the rings. She re-created the font style from a popular movie with a craft knife and overlaid her edge-to-edge photo with journaling on a transparency.

Barb De Shaw, Short Hills, New Jersey

Supplies: Patterned paper (MOD—my own design); frame charm (Imagine It); letter stamp (PSX Design); navy and yellow cardstocks; ball chain; transparency; eyelets

Football

With this photo, Ivette wanted to document her son's interest in football while capturing just how small he is next to the ol' pigskin. She used her son's actual shoelaces to stitch football lacings through her page and sanded the edges of her photos to give them a rugged, classic look.

Ivette Valladares, Miami Lakes, Florida

Supplies: Patterned paper, snaps and leather frame (Making Memories); sticker letters (Sticker Studio); epoxy word stickers (Creative Imaginations); black cardstock; brads; shoelaces

Playing Hopscotch

Stephanie was surprised to leave her son playing with sidewalk chalks one day and come home to him playing a game of hopscotch. She gave her title a faux 3-D look by adding chalk around the edges of letter stickers.

Stephanie Rarick, Elmendorf Air Force Base, Alaska

Supplies: Patterned paper (Daisy D's, Li'l Davis Designs); letter stickers (Creative Imaginations); decorative paper clip (EK Success); letter stamps (Making Memories, PSX Design); sage, red, black and white cardstocks; chalk; black stamping ink; black pen

Jake really surprised me one day when he was on the driveway playing with his sidewalk chalks, he had Zach help him draw a hopscotch and then he started playing it! I guess he must have learned it at pre-school. He was really into playing it and hopped, skipped and jumped the day away! I love his little chicken legs and they are extra cute in his little red boots!
June 2003

Bike Tricks

With the training wheels still on, Tarri documents her son's love for doing tricks on his bike. Tarri covered a library pocket in olive cardstock and inserted journaling inside.

Tarri Botwinski, Grand Rapids, Michigan

Supplies: Patterned paper (KI Memories); sticker letters (EK Success); letter stamps (PSX Design); epoxy sticker (Creative Imaginations); celery and olive cardstocks; fibers; eyelets; black stamping ink; library pocket

E is for Emotions

emotion (e mo´shen) n. any specific feeling; any of various complex reactions

Not a Laughing Matter

To see her daughter pout, all Amy has to do is bring up her first "boyfriend"! She dry-brushed a metal frame, background paper, photo mats and her photo with acrylic paints for a coordinated, one-of-a-kind look.

Amy Stultz, Mooresville, Indiana

Supplies: Patterned papers (Mustard Moon, 7 Gypsies); metal frame (Making Memories); letter stickers (Creative Imaginations); plastic letters (Colorbök); label maker (Dymo); black and white cardstocks; cork; brads; acrylic paint

Fear Factor

Chuck E. Cheese is every little kid's playground, right? Not for poor Kaeleigh, who is terrified of the big mouse himself. Ralonda added walnut ink to the centers of standard metal-rimmed tags and inked the edges to blend them in to the rest of the layout.

Ralonda Heston, Murfreesboro, Tennessee

Supplies: Patterned paper (Chatterbox); printed twill (www.lumpystuff.com); slide mount (www.mytreasurequest.com); metal letters and photo clips (Making Memories); rubber stamp (Impress Rubber Stamps); cardstock letters (Foofala); plastic letters (Remember When); brick cardstock; cord; tag; brads; brown stamping ink; walnut ink

High Maintenance

Kris' shot of her son's T-shirt sums up the demeanor of this challenging 3-year-old! Specific examples of Dylan's high maintenance behavior are charmingly strung together in a mini book under the color photo. Kris photocopied a page from a dictionary to serve as a background for the mini book.

Kris Gillespie, Friendswood, Texas

Supplies: Letter stamps, tags and bead chain (Making Memories); red, black and white cardstocks; black stamping ink; eyelets; foam tape

Laugh a Little Each Day

Shannon has never before or since been able to capture this same smile and uninhibited laughter with her camera, so she made sure her digital design centered on the photos. She cropped out the background of the focal-point photo before placing it and used a photo of her deck railing for the wood texture behind the title.

Shannon Freeman, Bellingham, Washington

Supplies: Drawing program (MicroGrafx Draw); paint program (Microsoft Paint)

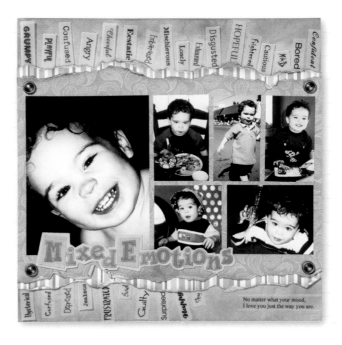

Mixed Emotions

Samatha was able to incorporate a variety of random snapshots for this page. She typed different emotions on the computer and changed the fonts and sizes to reflect the mood of each emotion.

Samantha Walker, Battle Ground, Washington

Supplies: Patterned paper (Chatterbox); decorative brads (Making Memories); letter stamps (Stampin' Up!); sand cardstock; vellum; brown stamping ink

Pure Joy

Tonya showcased this photo as a reminder of how happy, loving, silly and yes, joyful, her little girl could be. Inspired by the popular art of artist Roy Lichenstein, she included a poster-ized version of the original on this computer-generated page.

Tonya Doughty, Wenatchee, Washington

Supplies: Image-editing software (Adobe Photoshop)

Curiosity

Rusted industrial metal and a sweet boy's face make a wonderful study in contrasts on this colorful layout. Shari used mesh, screw-head snaps, a steel grate slide mount and license-plate letter stickers to carry through the industrial style of the photo setting.

Shari Schwalbe, Coral Springs, Florida

Supplies: Patterned paper and letter stickers (Paper Loft); screw-head snaps, photo anchors and photo corners (Making Memories); slide mount (Deluxe Designs); red cardstock; mesh; transparency; brads

Stetson

Natalie used a medium-format camera to shoot these photos for a class assignment, then chose a layout that would showcase their square shape. She came up with descriptions of her brother Stetson using the letters of his name to form a creative title.

Natalie Blake, Middletown, Ohio

Supplies: Patterned paper (Amscan); tag template (C-Thru Ruler); letter stickers (Creative Imaginations); leaf punches (All Night Media); square buttons (Hillcreek Designs); navy, slate and metallic pewter cardstocks; vellum; square punches; thread

First Day of School

It's the first day of "big school," and this little guy's expression says it all. Lisa swiped textured paper with acrylic paint, then added various letter types over it to help the title stand out.

Lisa Mote, Murfreesboro, Tennessee

Supplies: Patterned paper, page pebbles and rub-on words and letters (Making Memories); waffle paper (Creative Imaginations); letter stamps (Postmodern Design, PSX Design); cardstock letters (Foofala); index tab (7 Gypsies); metal stencil letter (Li'l Davis Designs); sage cardstock; metal clip; brads; acrylic paint; library card pocket; tag; date stamp; ribbon; brown stamping ink; black pen

Adult Swim Pout

Kelli's son Kevin channels the spirit of every kid who has ever had to sit by the side of the pool and wait for adult swim time to end. Kelli printed various details on a transparency, cut them out and adhered them to metal tags to make it look as if the tags were engraved that way.

Kelli Noto, Centennial, Colorado

Supplies: Patterned paper (American Crafts); metal tags (Happy Hammer); die-cut letters (QuicKutz); tan and navy cardstocks; brads; transparency

Tomorrow Is a New Day

Joy reminds her daughter (and herself) that whenever she feels blue or disappointed, tomorrow is a new day and a fresh start. She created her own patterned paper by printing the days of the week on cardstock and downloaded an image of clouds from Microsoft Gallery for an accent.

Joy Bollinger, Midlothian, Virginia

Supplies: Patterned paper and letter stickers (Creative Imaginations); brad letters (Colorbök); navy cardstock; ribbon; foam tape

Bottled Feelings

When the rest of the kids at the park were running, laughing and playing, Brandon took a few minutes to just sit and think. Martha captured this moment on film. She used old bottle caps to continue the theme of her patterned paper and symbolize her wish that she could uncap her son's thoughts during this quiet moment.

Martha Crowther, Salem, New Hampshire

Supplies: Patterned papers (Me & My Big Ideas, Rusty Pickle); fabric envelope (Li'l Davis Designs); coins (EK Success); stickers (Pebbles); black cardstock; black stamping ink; eyelets; foam tape; bottle caps; transparency; walnut ink

F is for Friends

friend (frend´) n. a person attached to another by feelings of affection

Best Buddies

As twins, these brothers share a special, unique friendship, which Kimberly captured on this spread. Colorful buttons, slide mounts, patterned paper and vellum keep the layout bright and playful.

Kimberly Kett, St. Catharines, Ontario, Canada

Supplies: Patterned paper, stickers, letter stickers and buttons (SEI); printed vellum (Kopp Design); rub-on word (Making Memories); circle punch; brads; slide mounts

Hands-Down, My Favorite Playmate

At the park one day, Teri realized that her children were truly each other's favorite playmates, as these joyful photos so powerfully attest. She used strokes of acrylic paint to emphasize key words in the title and journaling.

Teri Fode, Carmichael, California

Supplies: Patterned papers (Colors by Design, Making Memories, Wordsworth); wire mesh and photo clips (Making Memories); wire hands (Westrim); foam letter stamps (Duncan); letter stamps (Hero Arts); blue cardstock; vellum; fibers; brads; acrylic paints; black stamping ink; chalk

Siblings...Friends

Sometimes you don't have to see faces to capture a tender moment, as Valerie's focal-point photo demonstrates. Valerie stamped, embossed with silver powder and trimmed several frames for descriptive words to coordinate with metal-rimmed tags.

Valerie Barton, Flowood, Mississippi

Supplies: Patterned paper (Paper Loft); silver-rimmed tags (Making Memories); letter stickers (Mrs. Grossman's); stamps (All Night Media); brown cardstock; fibers; silver embossing powder; clear stamping ink; walnut ink

Best Friends

Brianne and Brynlin are inseparable, and Toni immortalizes their special friendship on this creative page. Blue stamping ink was applied to various elements across the page to reflect the painted look of the background paper.

Toni Boucha, Spring, Texas

Supplies: Patterned paper (Karen Foster Design, Pebbles); cork letters (Creative Imaginations); letter tiles (Card Connection); stamps (Hero Arts); tan cardstock; metal-rimmed tags; silk flower; button; fibers; staples; blue stamping ink

A True Friend

Adult friendships deserve to be showcased too, as Cheryl has done on this collaged page. She added stamping ink to help all papers blend together well and hand wrote a simple quote for the page's journaling.

Cheryl Manz, Paulding, Ohio

Supplies: Patterned papers (7 Gypsies, Daisy D's, K & Company, Me & My Big Ideas, MOD—my own design); rub-on word (Making Memories); tag; black stamping ink; ribbon; black pen

Friends

Learning about friendship is a big step in the process of growing up, and Teri-Lynn documented this experience for her oldest daughter. She created a digital background to mimic the stripes in her daughter's bathing suit and dialed down the opacity of her title letters to allow the background pattern to show through.

Teri-Lynn Masters, Truro, Nova Scotia, Canada

Supplies: Image-editing software (PaintShop Pro by Jasc)

Pals Make the Best Friends

These two really love to ham it up for the camera, allowing Cynthia to get some great shots of their relationship in a garage studio. She adhered scraps of patterned and solid papers at different angles to create a lively photo mat.

Cynthia Coulon, Provo, Utah

Supplies: Patterned papers (Paper Adventures, Patchwork Paper Design); twill ribbon and wood pieces (Scrapfindings); letter stamps (Hero Arts); tags; walnut ink; snaps; acrylic paint; stamping ink; sewing machine

Best Friend

Laura showed off some of the fabulous effects you can achieve on computer-generated layouts with this page about her son and his best friend. She first de-saturated her photos to make them all black-and-white, then added color back in by selecting different areas and adjusting the color balance to achieve the right tint.

Laura Lee Shirt, Sherwood Park, Alberta, Canada

Supplies: Text overlay (www.scrapbook-bytes.com); image-editing software

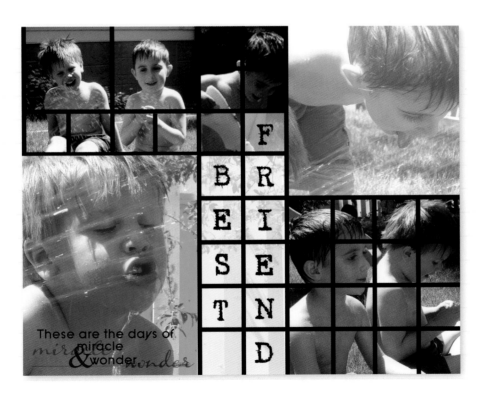

Soul Mates

This feminine spread celebrates a friendship that became even more special when one girl had to move. Since some of her patterned paper was printed on both sides, Mary tore out a window for her title, folded the paper back and stitched it down to allow the other pattern to show.

Mary Zimmer, New Baltimore, Michigan

Supplies: Patterned papers (K & Company); ribbon flower trim (Jo-Ann Fabrics); sage and pink cardstocks; jute; eyelets; lace trim; thread

Friendship

Megan and Jenna met through gymnastics, but soon a true friendship was born. Amy layered a number of downloaded backgrounds and elements to create this charming digital page.

Amy Edwards, Newark Valley, New York
Photo: Tracey Cupp, Newark Valley, New York

Supplies: Image-editing software (Adobe Photoshop); paper, hemp, photo mat, tag, eyelet and lettering images (www.ddecd.com); staples and text overlay (www.scrapbook-bytes.com)

Youth

It's a wonderful mystery what secrets transpire between two little girls at play. Rachael combined alphabet stamps and her own handwriting for journaling that coordinates with a preprinted transparency.

Rachael Giallongo
Auburn, New Hampshire

Supplies: Patterned paper (Close To My Heart); letter stamps (EK Success); slide mount (www.pic-mount.com); printed transparency (Creative Imaginations); label maker (Dymo); pink cardstock; tack; ribbon; acrylic paint; metal-rimmed tag; foam tape

Friends for Life

Christine created this layout to remind herself of a time when her daughters got along well. She stretched a ribbon behind a vellum title to separate it from the background and add color.

Christine Traversa, Joliet, Illinois

Supplies: Patterned paper and die cuts (DieCuts with a View); printed vellum (C-Thru Ruler); date stamp; black stamping inks; ribbon; vellum

F is for Flowers

flower (flou´er) n. a plant cultivated for its blossom

Little Boys Are Common Miracles

Monochromatic dandelion patterned paper was the perfect complement for this photo, which Ginger printed in sepia. She created corrugated paper by running her photo mat through a crimper and adding walnut ink to bring out texture.

Ginger McSwain, Cary, North Carolina

Supplies: Patterned paper (Masterpiece Studios); tag and epoxy letter sticker (K & Company); white and khaki cardstocks; brown and rust stamping inks; jute

My First Flowers

There is nothing quite as sweet as the first time a child brings you flowers, even if it's a bag full of dandelions floating in water! Jackie changed this photo of her son to black-and-white, leaving the dandelions in his bag in color to emphasize them.

Jackie Siperko, Dallas, Pennsylvania

Supplies: Patterned paper (Pebbles); fawn cardstock; brads; floss; ribbon; black stamping ink

Spring

Lisa wanted these vivid photos of her daughter and spring flowers to really stand out, so she kept her background colors light and neutral. Fibers, label holders and stencil letters were chosen to further the neutral appearance of the layout.

Lisa Turley, Chesapeake, Virginia

Supplies: Patterned paper (Scenic Route Paper Co.); letter stamps, date stamp and label holders (Making Memories); stencil letters (Autumn Leaves); buckle charms (Jest Charming); fibers; brads; brown stamping ink

Spring

Lisa chose vibrant, energetic patterns for a layout that really shouts "spring." She applied white acrylic paint with a dry brush around the page border and painted the metal letter stencils to coordinate.

Lisa Turley, Chesapeake, Virginia

Supplies: Patterned papers, buckle and acrylic stickers (KI Memories); stencil letters (Colorbök); white cardstock; fibers; pink stamping ink; acrylic paint

Summer

Sights

Favorite Summer Sights

bees buzzing
flowers blooming
afternoon showers
ice cream trucks
kids in sprinklers
rainbows
arts and crafts shows

A beautiful afternoon enjoying The Festival of Flowers at Park Seed Company in Greenwood, South Carolina. June 21, 2003

Summer Sights

Rhonda listed the sights and sounds that are quintessentially summer to her, and illustrated them with her photos. She called attention to specific sections of the photos by using a page pebble and vellum with a square cut from the center.

Rhonda Buyck, Florence, South Carolina

Supplies: Epoxy letter stickers and page pebble (Creative Imaginations); orange, pumpkin and turquoise cardstocks; eyelets; ribbon; vellum; extra thick embossing powder; circle punch

f

Spring 2003

What says spring more than a beautiful little girl in an Easter dress in front of a garden full of flowers? The title tag lifts up to reveal Mom's thoughts about seeing her little girl all gussied up for Easter Sunday.

Kathryn Allen, Hamilton, Ohio

Supplies: Preprinted vellum (EK Success); letter stamps (Hero Arts); shaped eyelets (source unknown); green, red and white cardstocks; red stamping ink; fibers; black pen

Bright As Flowers

When the weather starts to warm and flowers come to life, Barb cannot resist the siren call of her camera. Preprinted transparencies are the only accents needed on this layout awash with spring color and beauty.

Barb Hogan, Cincinnati, Ohio

Supplies: Patterned paper (American Crafts); preprinted transparency (Creative Imaginations); vellum; brads; black stamping ink

Du Är Blomman...

The joy of flowers is the same in every language. In Swedish, Theresa's page reads "You are the flower. I am the gardener." She inked the edges of punched leaves for a more sophisticated look.

Theresa Lundstroem, Skelleftea, Sweden

Supplies: Patterned paper (Karen Foster Design); silk flowers (Making Memories); kraft and light green card-stocks; snaps; lace; leaf punch; brown stamping ink

A Summer of Discovery

Debra created detailed 3-D flower embellishments by stamping and embossing two versions of each flower and painting them with watercolors and metallic pigment powders. She then silhouette cut each flower, cut sections from some of them and layered the sections over the first stamped flower with foam adhesive. To add journaling while still focusing on page design, Debra printed journaling on vellum and rolled it into a scroll.

Debra Hendren, Royal Oak, Michigan

Supplies: Preprinted vellum (EK Success); metal frame, metal squares, eyelet letters, and letter charms (Making Memories); letter stamps (Hero Arts); flower stamps (Stamp Pad Company); metallic pigment powders (Jacquard Products); beads (Beader's Paradise); buttons (Junkitz); green, forest, brick and orange cardstocks; orange mulberry paper; fibers; button; eyelets; wire; embroidery floss; clear embossing ink; embossing powder; charm; foam tape; watercolor paints

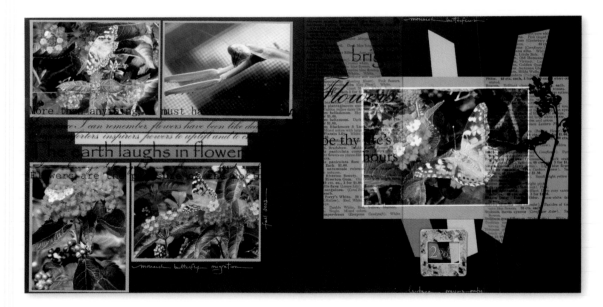

The Earth Laughs in Flowers

A black background brings out the vibrant colors in Barb's photos. For embellishment, Barb sandwiched a transparency between two halves of a slide mount, added sticker letters and decorated the mount with beads, tiny glass marbles and extra thick embossing powder.

Barb Hogan, Cincinnati, Ohio

Supplies: Preprinted transparency (Creative Imaginations); sticker letters (SEI); black, yellow, pink, red and olive cardstocks; beads; tiny glass marbles; clear embossing ink; extra thick embossing powder; slide mount; brads

Wildflowers

How can you resist a little boy who asks you to put a dandelion in your hair because it makes you look pretty? Cassandra tucked her journaling behind the main photo, and used different colors and sizes of brads to anchor the top hinge.

Cassandra McDaniel, Bellevue, Washington

Supplies: Patterned papers (Me & My Big Ideas, Provo Craft, 7 Gypsies); deco brad, safety pin, paper tags, metal letters and rub-on word (Making Memories); definition sticker (Pebbles); typewriter key letters (Colorbök); plaque (K & Company); letter stamps (Ma Vinci's Reliquary); mustard cardstock; silk flower; brads; jump rings; date stamp; hinges; ribbon; black and brown stamping inks; heart beads

Beautiful

The fact that she was wearing a fancy dress didn't stop Hailey when the water hose came out. Tiny clear beads adhered to the photograph with clear lacquer emphasize the shower of water. Flower accents were handmade from paper ribbon, wire, fibers and beads to echo the flowers on Hailey's dress.

Renae Clark, Mazomanie, Wisconsin

Supplies: Patterned paper (Karen Foster Design); beads (Darice); paper ribbon (Emagination Crafts); green and brick cardstocks; vellum; fibers; clear lacquer

G is for Glasses and Goggles

glass•es (glas´ ez) n. devices worn to protect the eyes or improve the vision
gog•gles (gäg´ elz) n. devices worn to protect the eyes beneath water

Sipping Soda

Car trips on summer days require two things—a cool soda and a cool pair of shades. A real bottle cap, pounded flat, found permanent salvation from the garbage as a flashy embellishment on this page.

Raechelle Bellus, Spokane Valley, Washington

Supplies: Patterned paper (Rusty Pickle); leather flower and label holder (Making Memories); word sticker (7 Gypsies); letter stickers (Creative Imaginations); sticker (Pebbles); chocolate, brown, khaki and white cardstocks; fibers; brown stamping ink; bottle cap; staples; brad

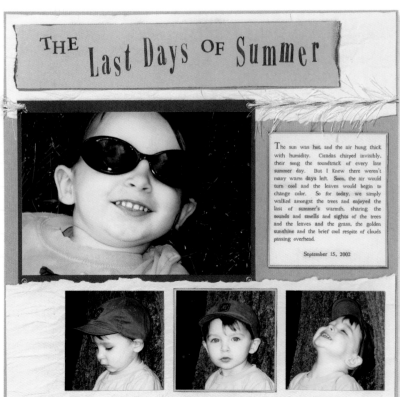

The Last Days of Summer

Jennifer couldn't help but capture her son lying in the grass with his shades on during one of the last moments of summer. She highlighted selected words in her journaling with chalk in a color that coordinates with the title block.

Jennifer Adams Donnelly, Crestwood, Illinois

Supplies: Letter stamps (All Night Media, Club Scrap); blue, marigold, orange and brown cardstocks; fibers; eyelets; chalk; brown and black stamping inks

Emma Is Cool

What does a 1-month-old do to look cool? Wear oversized shades, of course! Jess was amazed by how tiny her newborn daughter was compared to her hand, so she had the photo enlarged to life-size to capture how tiny she really was.

Jess Atkinson, Harrisburg, Pennsylvania

Supplies: Patterned paper and word circle (KI Memories); letter stamps (PSX Design); green cardstock; black stamping ink

Canine Cool

A pet wearing sunglasses always makes for a humorous layout. Ann "stamped" her digital background paper with a custom eyeglass brush in image-editing software to echo the page's eyewear theme.

Ann Hetzel Gunkel, Chicago, Illinois

Supplies: Image-editing software (Adobe Photoshop); letter stamp images (www.scrapbook-bytes.com); eyeglass brush, ribbons, eyelet, crepe paper and background images (www.designbutcher.com)

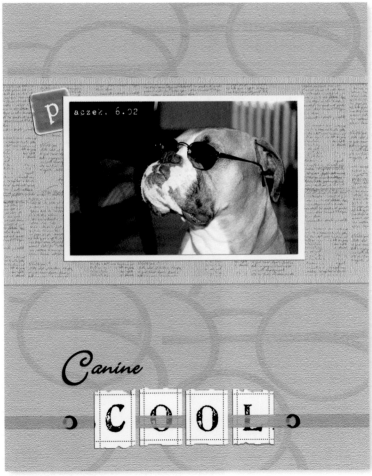

View the World...

Sam accidentally smudged ink on a tag, so she turned it into a fun embellishment by adding her own and her son's fingerprints to cover up the error. A corner accent made from mesh, a safety pin and a letter tag help create a point of focus.

Sam Cousins, Trumbull, Connecticut

Supplies: Patterned paper and tag (SEI); rub-on words, letter tag, and safety pin (Making Memories); letter stamps (PSX Design); sticker letters (Wordsworth); wine charm (TJ Maxx); round letter sticker (Creative Imaginations); mesh (Magic Mesh); white cardstock; black stamping ink; brads

Laughter

This quirky portrait gives a glimpse into Cheryl's personality, glasses and all. She painted stencil letters and a word plaque, then swiped some of the paint off to let the shiny metal show through.

Cheryl Manz, Paulding, Ohio

Supplies: Patterned papers (Design Originals, Karen Foster Design, SEI); letter stencils (Colorbök); plaque (Li'l Davis Designs); tan cardstock; jute; acrylic paint; black stamping ink

Treasure

Children should always see the world through rose-colored glasses—sunglasses, that is! Rebecca only had white rub-on letters and wanted black ones for this page, so she traced the word "treasure" with a black pen.

Rebecca Avila, Temecula, California

Supplies: Patterned papers (Club Scrap, Doodlebug Design); textured strips (Chatterbox); word rub-ons (All My Memories, Making Memories); white and black markers; brads; charm; clear beads; wire; lace; heart eyelet; black stamping ink; ribbon

An Open Book...

A child with a love of books is a precious thing, and Shannon records her eyeglass-clad reader with humorous journaling. She enlarged a photograph of books, then converted it to black-and-white and split the photo in half to create a border on this digital layout.

Shannon Freeman, Bellingham, Washington

Supplies: Drawing program (MicroGrafx Draw)

Spring Fever

Spring break meant a trip to Disney World and a new pair of "glamour girl" sunglasses for Kay's daughter. Kay matted postage stamp embellishments and sprinkled them across her spread to coordinate with her pink, lavender and green color scheme.

Kay Rogers, Midland, Michigan

Supplies: Patterned paper and stamp stickers (K & Company); flower sticker (Pebbles); plastic window and nails (Chatterbox); rub-on words and silk flowers (Making Memories); pink, lavender and green cardstocks; fibers; green and purple stamping inks

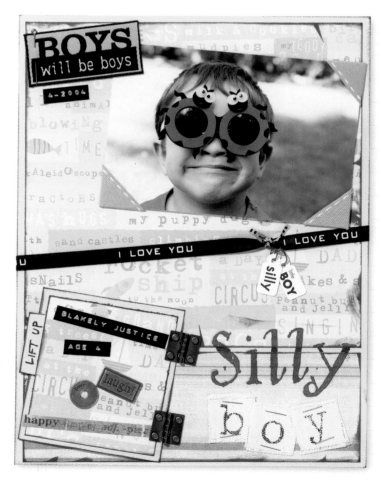

Silly Boy

Crazy glasses seem to demand that their picture be taken, especially on a little boy with a big sense of humor. One of Cassandra's page elements is hidden journaling, which she included beneath a small hinged door, decorated with metal accents and label tape.

Cassandra McDaniel, Bellevue, Washington

Supplies: Patterned papers (K & Company, Me & My Big Ideas); photo corners, woven labels, printed ribbon, word tags, safety pin, word washer, hinges, and ribbon charm (Making Memories); canvas letters (Li'l Davis Designs); definition sticker (Pebbles); word charm (K & Company); letter stamps (Ma Vinci's Reliquary); light blue and maize cardstocks; ribbon; jump rings; snaps; label tape; black stamping ink; staples; black pen

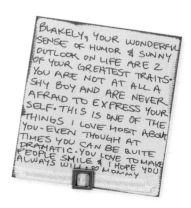

Through Your Eyes

Robin documented her daughter's optometrist visit and her feelings about her getting glasses for the first time. She included lots of memorabilia and highlighted the C (for Claire) on an eye chart she downloaded from the Internet.

Robin Hohenstern, Brooklyn Park, Minnesota

Supplies: Patterned paper and tack (Chatterbox); letter stamps (Hero Arts); cream cardstock; circle punch; eyelets; string; transparencies; photo corners; paper clip; trim; thread; magnifying lens; brown stamping ink

Fly

Karen remembers when her father learned to fly—and how scared she felt as the plane left the ground after he promised they were only going to taxi down the runway! For the title, Karen printed out letters, traced them on faux metal paper, cut them out and attached screen mesh to the backs with eyelets. She sanded the fronts of letters for a brushed metal look.

Karen Robinson, Cumberland, Rhode Island

Supplies: Patterned paper (Rusty Pickle); faux metal paper (Magic Scraps); hinges (Making Memories); metal screen mesh (Scrapyard 329); gray and smoke cardstocks; eyelets; transparency; black stamping ink

Come Out and Play

April's daughter begged for these goggles, then decided that her frog float really needed to wear them instead. Round conchos, circle clips and eyelets in place of some "O"s in her journaling mimic the shape of the eyewear.

April Kleinfeldt, Greensboro, North Carolina

Supplies: Patterned paper (Doodlebug Design); conchos (Scrapworks); rub-on words (Making Memories); aqua and sage cardstocks; vellum; fibers; ribbon; circle clips; eyelets; jewelry tags; acrylic paint; blue stamping ink

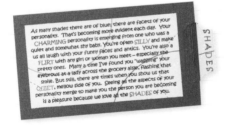

Shades of Blue, Shades of You

A play on words in Patti's title describe her son's glasses, color of his eyes and his personality. An index divider tab leads to hidden journaling tucked behind the main photo. Metal stencils embossed with black powder spell this charming young man's name.

Patti Milazzo, Lexington, South Carolina

Supplies: Patterned paper and stickers (KI Memories); metal stencil letters (Card Connection); blue cardstock; eyelets; embossing powder; embossing ink; divider tab; date stamp; stamping ink; slide mount

Summer

Swim goggles are synonymous with summertime fun in the pool and provide some great photo opportunities. For her title, Lisa transferred a rub-on word onto a paint chip, then swiped it with ink to turn the title gray.

Lisa Mote, Murfreesboro, Tennessee

Supplies: Printed vellum and tab (KI Memories); paint chip (PM designs); word stamp (Wordsworth); stamp (Stampotique Originals); rub-on word (Making Memories); epoxy letter stickers (Creative Imaginations); light blue cardstock; circle clip; ribbon; brads; black stamping ink

Laugh Louder

Kelly never wants her son to forget to laugh and have fun, as her page title suggests. She used rub-on letters to create the two "laughs" in her title, then printed a transparency with the rest of the words and layered it on top.

Kelly Rakow, Elgin, Illinois

Supplies: Patterned papers and tags (KI Memories); rub-on letters (Autumn Leaves); black and white cardstocks; transparency; black stamping ink

H is for Hats

hat (hat) n. a covering for the head, usually with a brim and a crown

Begin...

This spread takes on a very old-fashioned feel with the combination of black-and-white matte-finished photos, antiqued papers and the classic baseball cap-clad little boy in the snow. Collage techniques using various media decorate the tags behind the photos.

Linda Albrecht, St. Peter, Minnesota

Supplies: Patterned papers (Hot Off The Press, K & Company, Provo Craft); stickers (K & Company); star eyelets (Westrim); tag stickers (EK Success); snowflake charms (Jo-Ann Fabrics); wire; ribbon; glass pebbles; embossing powder; brown stamping ink; brads; transparency

Grandpa's Handmade Hats

What better way to entertain a couple of energetic grandsons than making them old-fashioned newspaper hats? While the 4-year-old was busy taking a photo of Grandma wearing his hat, Grandpa made an extra mini hat to adorn this page.

Sue Fields, South Whitley, Indiana

Supplies: Patterned papers, die cuts and slide mount (Design Originals); scrabble letters (Card Connection); black, red and yellow cardstocks; ribbon; newspaper; black stamping ink

Tubing

Martha captures one of the joys of snow in these photos. She inserted smaller photos into slide mounts to serve as a border.

Martha Crowther, Salem, New Hampshire

Supplies: Patterned paper (KI Memories); orange, sky and black cardstocks; fibers; stickers; slide mounts

Slow Down...

Warm hats, coats, gloves and cold-rosy cheeks and noses are the essence of wintertime. Martha found a bit of gift wrap twine on clearance and used it as an innovative frame for her focal-point photo.

Martha Crowther, Salem, New Hampshire

Supplies: Patterned paper (Danielle Donaldson); tag (Cut-It-Up); stickers (EK Success); purple, burgundy and pumpkin cardstocks; fibers; corner rounder; vellum; snowflake twine

Yummy!

Sepia-toned photographs and a boy in a cowboy hat make the perfect combination for this rustic layout. Amy punched squares from some of the photos, letting the distressed paper mats show through. The punched pieces were matted and placed beside the original photos as accents.

Amy Hatch, Ogden, Utah

Supplies: Patterned paper and printed tags (Paper Loft); frame and cut-out (My Mind's Eye); cream cardstock; square punch; fibers; eyelets; vellum; chalk

The Game

When you're all bundled up complete with Scooby-Doo hat and strapped in a car seat, what is there to do while Mom runs errands? The Game! Tarri used this layout to document the rules of a car game that she and her children made up one day. Staples attached the rules to the page and accent the photo mat and background.

Tarri Botwinski, Grand Rapids, Michigan

Supplies: Patterned papers and tacks (Chatterbox); letter stickers (Sticker Studio); letter stamps (PSX Design); black stamping ink; staples

Hats Off to You at 5

A little girl playing with a stack of hats makes a great photo opportunity. Robin's favorite photo of her daughter in a hat came out slightly blurry, so she disguised the fuzziness by printing it on canvas and fraying the edges.

Robin Hohenstern, Brooklyn Park, Minnesota

Supplies: Patterned papers (Chatterbox, Design Originals); embossed paper (Lasting Impressions); patterned vellum, flower tacks, rivet and letter stickers (Chatterbox); letter stamps (Hero Arts, PSX Design); cream and olive cardstocks; circle punches; date stamp; number stencil; canvas paper; tag; sewing machine; black stamping ink

Love Your Dreams...

A vintage-style hat and a sepia-toned photo add a classic look to this dreamy photo. Theresa ran a strip of tan cardstock through her label maker to create the words below the photo. She included some of her daughter's drawings and dreams in the mini book on the tag.

Theresa Lundstroem, Skelleftea, Sweden

Supplies: Patterned papers (K & Company, Karen Foster Design, Making Memories); wing stamps (Making Memories); corner embellishment (Daisy D's); cream cardstock; decorative scissors; heart punch; charms; lace; brown stamping ink; string; sewing machine

Like Daddy

Green flower accents illustrate a cute observation Nancy's daughter made about her green eyes. Nancy enlarged one photo, printed it in black-and-white and hand-tinted her daughter's eyes for emphasis.

Nancy Rogers, Baton Rouge, Louisiana

Supplies: Patterned paper (Karen Foster Design); tiny glass marbles (Magic Scraps); die-cut flowers (Sizzix); black, charcoal and gray cardstocks; floss; chalk; photo-tinting oils

What Do You Do in the Summertime?

The colors of Jodi's page mimic the colors of the hat in this darling baby photo. Jodi dry-embossed her photo mat and title strip for dimension and added more detail by stitching parts of the letters in "Summertime."

Jodi Millecam, Sandy, Utah
Photo: Kapture Kids

Supplies: Sticker letters (All My Memories); embossing template (source unknown); orange, pink and hot pink cardstocks; square brads; embroidery floss; foam tape

Reach High

Lisa chose photos of her visor-clad daughter to muse about the dreams she has for her. She brushed the edges of her background with acrylic paint to bring out the texture of the cardstock and highlight the words printed along the edges of her transparency.

Lisa Turley, Chesapeake, Virginia

Supplies: Preprinted transparency (Sarah Heidt Photo Craft); flower charm (www.memoriesoftherabbit.com); indigo and cream cardstocks; brads; embroidery floss; acrylic paint; black stamping ink

Snowmen

A dramatic enlargement of a lovingly crafted snowman complete with warm hat is the unequivocal focus of this simple page. Angela typed her title and used the WordArt feature to give it the wavy feeling of falling snow.

Angela Marvel, Puyallup, Washington

Supplies: Patterned paper (Hot Off The Press); black, white and red cardstocks

True Hero

Kris created this spread to remind her son that anything is possible with an embroidered Peter Pan hat and a little imagination. She joined her smaller photos together with jump rings and charms swiped with acrylic paint. A feather like the one in her son's cap is sandwiched between the background and a transparency printed with a quote.

Kris Gillespie, Friendswood, Texas

Supplies: Letter charm and stamps (Making Memories); zipper pulls (All My Memories); printed slide mounts (Creative Imaginations); patterned papers (source unknown); letter stencil; feather; transparency; acrylic paint, black stamping ink; ribbon; brads; jump rings

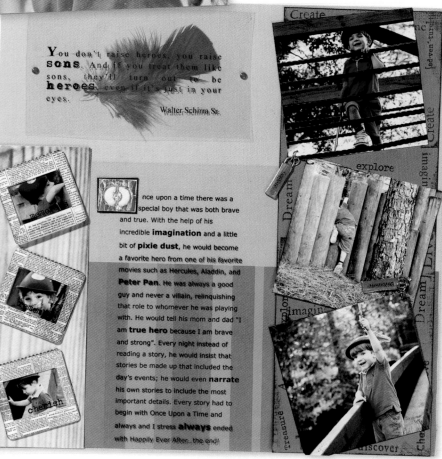

You don't raise heroes, you raise **sons**. And if you treat them like sons, they'll turn out to be **heroes** even if it's just in your eyes.

Walter Schirra Sr.

nce upon a time there was a special boy that was both brave and true. With the help of his incredible **imagination** and a little bit of **pixie dust**, he would become a favorite hero from one of his favorite movies such as Hercules, Aladdin, and **Peter Pan**. He was always a good guy and never a villain, relinquishing that role to whomever he was playing with. He would tell his mom and dad "I am **true hero** because I am brave and strong". Every night instead of reading a story, he would insist that stories be made up that included the day's events; he would even **narrate** his own stories to include the most important details. Every story had to begin with Once Upon a Time and always and I stress **always** ended with Happily Ever After...the end!

Hey There Jordy Girl

A simple hat can add so much character and whimsy to a traditionally styled portrait. A variety of metal accents, including letter tiles, photo corners, quote plaque and ribbon charm unify Wendy's design.

Wendy Bickford, Antelope, California
Photos: Kelli Dickenson, Des Moines, Iowa

Supplies: Patterned papers (Scenic Route Paper Co.); ribbon charm, quote plaque, photo corners and letter tiles (Making Memories); tan cardstock; transparency; ribbon; brads; brown stamping ink

Princess

No princess dress-up outfit is complete without a sparking, beaded tiara. The bottom of the focal-point photo was torn and coated with a subtle shimmer of iridescent embossing powder to mimic the sequined dress and crown in the photos.

Nancy Rogers, Baton Rouge, Louisiana

Supplies: Patterned paper (Anna Griffin); ribbon charm, letter tag, and flower charms (Making Memories); rhinestone brads (Magic Scraps); pocket and tag templates (Deluxe Designs); navy, blue and cream cardstocks; ribbon; silk flower; eyelet; embossing ink; extra thick embossing powder

Madison

Madison couldn't get enough of these fabulous sets and fun vintage clothing and hats, so the photographer ended up taking more than 100 photos! Then it was her mom's turn to have fun antiquing this page by stamping her daughter's name in red, dry-brushing acrylic paint over it, then sanding it so that the red letters peeked through.

Lily Goldsmith, Orlando, Florida
Photo: Ashton Photography, Oviedo, Florida

Supplies: Foam letter stamps, decorative brads, metal tag and copper letter tiles (Making Memories); letter stamps (PSX Design); photo corners (K & Company); clay word (Li'l Davis Designs); watch stamp (Rubber Stampede); tan, olive and berry cardstocks; ribbon; envelope; twill tape; square brads; printed twill; corrugated paper; button; staples; acrylic paints; brown and red stamping inks; brown pen

Patriotic Attitude

This charming 3-year-old has all the patriotic attitude she needs, right up to her oversized stovepipe hat. Christine trimmed a star out of patterned paper and adhered it over a metal plaque with foam tape for an embellishment that stands out.

Christine Traversa, Joliet, Illinois

Supplies: Patterned papers (Club Scrap, Sticker Studio); letter stickers (K & Company); metal plaque (Making Memories); date stamp; chalk pencils; fibers; ribbon; red stamping ink; foam tape

The Love of a Pirate

Add a black felt hat, and a little boy offering a dandelion is suddenly a pirate showing off his softer side. Melanie cut her photo mat from a second sheet of patterned paper so the design lined up precisely with the background paper.

Melanie Bruner, Knoxville, Tennessee

Supplies: Patterned paper (K & Company); foam letter stamps (Making Memories); black cardstock; acrylic paint; date stamp; black stamping ink; transparency

h

H is for Horizons

ho•ri•zon (he ri´ zon) n. the line where the sky seems to meet the earth

Moment of Perfection

Perfection is indeed reflected in this serene photo of a couple gazing out at the sunset-tinged horizon. A slide mount wrapped in ribbon adds a simple, elegant touch.

Amanda Goodwin, Munroe Falls, Ohio

Supplies: Patterned paper (Chatterbox); rub-on words (Making Memories); glitter flakes (Magic Scraps); heart charm; ribbon; slide mount

Peace

Inspired by a layout she saw on www.twopeas inabucket.com, Arlene created this peaceful computer-generated page for her sister. She used diffuse glow and soft light filters on her sister's portrait to soften it and keep the focus on the center photo, one that her sister took.

Arlene Santos, Mililani, Hawaii

Supplies: Image-editing software (Adobe Photoshop); butterfly brush (www.truly-sarah.com)

Psalm 119:114

To create a page complementing a Scripture from the book of Psalms, Daphne snapped this incredible photo of a field of safflowers leading up to a lone tree on the horizon. She cut a frame out of gold-accented patterned paper and mounted the beginning of the verse inside it.

Daphne Nunez, Bayside, New York

Supplies: Patterned papers (K & Company, Sandylion); brown and pumpkin cardstocks; vellum; eyelets; gold cord; embroidery floss; copper stamping ink; embossing powder

Solitude

A quiet boat with billowing sails and a clear sea all the way to the horizon combine in this peaceful portrait of solitude. Missy echoed the main colors in her photo when choosing cardstocks and edged each cardstock piece with stamping ink to give it definition.

Missy Partridge, Berlin, Maryland

Supplies: Rub-on word (Making Memories); tacks (Bazzill); cream, white, blue and sapphire cardstocks; black stamping ink

Sea, Sky, Sand and Daddy

Katie took these photos of her husband and children staring off toward the endless sea. She split her journaling into sections, matching each part to a different photo.

Katie Bigney, Carmichael, California

Supplies: Beach embellishments (EK Success); blue and navy cardstocks; vellum; fibers; mesh; brads; glass beads; brown stamping ink

Wonder

There's something magical that happens when a child experiences the beach for the first time. Shelley extended the horizon in the photo across the page by using cardstock overlaid with vellum, then detailing with a black pen. She spelled her daughter's name in letter stickers on a shell they found on the beach.

Shelley Rankin, Fredericton, New Brunswick, Canada

Supplies: Patterned paper (Hot Off The Press); definition sticker and epoxy words (Making Memories); mesh (Magenta); pebbles (Creative Imaginations); letter stickers (source unknown); sand, white, red and blue cardstocks; corrugated paper; metal-rimmed tag; jute; white pen; seashells

Our Horizon

An enlarged photo effectively echoes the expansiveness of the sunset sky, which is Kimberly's favorite part of camping. For a simple accent, she cut a thin strip of cardstock and lined it edge-to-edge with tiny rectangles of colored cardstocks to create stripes.

Kimberly Lund, Wichita, Kansas

Supplies: Letter stickers (Deluxe Designs); peach, burgundy, sapphire and pumpkin cardstocks

Creating Memories

A silhouette against a sparkling, endless sea makes for a dramatic photo, especially when enlarged. A gold wine charm serves as an effective, eye-catching embellishment near the title while seashells adhered to the photo mat lend texture.

Michele Woods, Reynoldsburg, Ohio

Supplies: Definition sticker (Making Memories); wine glass charm (Montage Designs); black, brown and white cardstocks; seashells

Love on the Horizon

Holly wanted to emphasize the beautiful sunset in one of her honeymoon photos, so she enlarged it to 8 x 10" and used the enlargement as the frame behind her matted photo. She included a small picture of another sunset in a frame charm to accent her journaling.

Holly VanDyne, Mansfield, Ohio

Supplies: Textured paper (Provo Craft); preprinted transparency (My Minds Eye); rub-on letters (Making Memories); navy and white cardstocks; circle clip; ribbon; frame charm; staples

Shell Seekers

Sometimes a single photo captures the essence of an afternoon on the beach so perfectly, it's worth using twice. With image-editing software, Virginia scanned her original photo, enlarged and flipped it, converted it to sepia, lightened two areas for her title and journaling, added text and printed it on beige vellum.

Virginia Lincoln, Glen Rock, New Jersey

Supplies: Word charm (source unknown); button word (source unknown); white, tan and black cardstocks; image-editing software; mesh; eyelets; ribbon; vellum; metal tag; brush pen; embossing powder; wire

Taking a Hike

A panoramic photo really takes advantage of the beautiful scenery and sprawling horizon in this shot. Amy kept the colors neutral and the layout simple to let the single photo take center stage.

Amy Howe, Frisco, Texas

Supplies: Patterned paper (Chatterbox); tan stamping ink

Come Sail Away With Me

A Caribbean island, a traditional 54-foot clipper, a clear, blue horizon and a loved one to share it with make for a great memory. And not a bad opportunity for Corinne to use the nautical stickers she'd had in her supplies for many years.

Corinne Lutter, Edmonton, Alberta, Canada

Supplies: Nautical stickers (Frances Meyer); red, white and navy cardstocks; vellum

i

I is for Insects

in•sect (in´ sekt´) n. popularly any arthropod, usually wingless

A Bee or Not a Bee?

Cherie created this layout to document her son's confusion between bees and harmless flies. She modified colors in her focal-point photo to keep the emphasis on the bee, and tied bits of ribbon to rickrack to dress up her border.

Cherie Ward, Colorado Springs, Colorado

Supplies: Patterned paper (Autumn Leaves); letter stamps (EK Success, Hero Arts, Ma Vinci's Reliquary); metal letter tag and silk flowers (Making Memories); label maker (Dymo); pink, green and white cardstocks; hand-made paper; tags; safety pin; ribbon; rickrack; brads; black and brown stamping inks; transparency

Walk...

For a girl who's fascinated with all creatures great and small, a puddle teeming with tadpoles and various insects is a treasure indeed. Nancy used a smorgasbord of font styles and type sizes to turn a quote into an attention-grabbing design element.

Nancy Thompson, Homer, New York

Supplies: Preprinted cut-outs (Pebbles); olive, sage and cream cardstocks; brads

Bug Knowledge

Amber admits that even she has learned a thing or two about bugs through her son's fascination with all insectlike critters. She stamped a butterfly, colored it with watercolor pencils and cut it out for a bright page accent.

Amber Crosby, Houston, Texas

Supplies: Patterned paper (K & Company); handmade paper (Jennifer Collection); twill tape and wooden circles (Scrapfindings); hinges, definition sticker and label holder (Making Memories); butterfly stamp (Stampin' Up!); letter stamps (PSX Design); leaf sticker (Pebbles); blue, green and brown cardstocks; acrylic paint; watercolor pencils; brads; black and brown stamping inks

Your fascination with bugs never ceases to amaze me. You love to play with your collection of toy bugs and never tire of looking at your bug book. The other day you saw a beetle in the driveway and then you told me that you had seen that type of bug in your book. I was quite impressed when you proudly showed me the very same bug in your book. We then had to read all about it, of course. I don't mind reading to you about bugs though. It is so wonderful for Mommy to see you excited about learning. Due to your fascination with bugs, Mommy has even learned a thing or two about them.

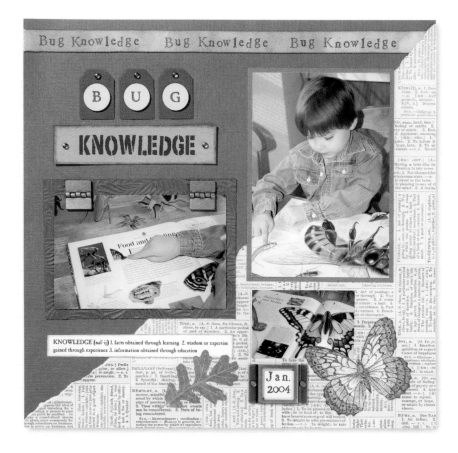

Close Encounters

These photos follow a child's thought process as he discovers his first giant slug, from tentative touch to a daring taste! Mary-Catherine added ink to wood veneer tape to create a frame. Title letters were made of plastic binding discs, sticker letters and a touch of clear lacquer.

Mary-Catherine Kropinski, Coquitlam, British Columbia, Canada

Supplies: Patterned papers (Creative Imaginations); handmade paper (Leapenhi Paper Design); mesh (Jest Charming); letter stickers (Provo Craft); letter stamps (PSX Design); plastic binding discs (Rollabind); forest green cardstock; fibers, laminate chip; black stamping ink; clear lacquer; wood veneer tape

True Colors of Spring

The butterfly and orchid exhibit is one of Kim's favorite places to visit in the spring. She stitched letters on fabric to form her title and printed several photos in a strip to mimic the look of a paint chip.

Kim Henkel, Oceanside, California

Supplies: Patterned paper (Chatterbox); handmade paper (www.BooksByHand.com); letter stamps (PSX Design); rectangle clip (Making Memories); brown cardstock; fabric; rickrack; fibers; embroidery floss; buttons; tags; ribbon; burlap; brown stamping inks

Nature

Sue's father was understandably proud of taking these vibrant butterfly shots, so she created this layout for him as a Father's Day gift. She inked the edges of torn vellum to give it a somewhat burnt look and help it stand out against the yellow background.

Sue Fields, South Whitley, Indiana
Photos: John VandenBerg, Fort Wayne, Indiana

Supplies: Patterned vellum and stickers (K & Company); square tag and printed ribbon (Making Memories); ribbon slide (Maya Road); printed vellum (DieCuts with a View); yellow and black cardstocks; ribbon; black stamping ink

Cicada Mania

The cicadas come out only once every 17 years, so it was definitely an event to document. Susan enlarged one photograph of cicadas in the trees for a background. She cut a small square from another photo and reattached it in the same place with foam tape to emphasize the cicada on her daughter's shoulder.

Susan Piepol, Rockville, Maryland

Supplies: Tags (Making Memories); green and orange cardstocks; fibers

Victoria Bug Zoo

Trudy describes her hatred of bugs on this page, and her eternal wonder at why she thought it was a good idea to chaperone her son's trip to the Bug Zoo. She transferred rub-on title letters onto bits of cardstock, inked the edges and raised a few of them up with foam tape for dimension.

Trudy Sigurdson, Victoria, British Columbia, Canada

Supplies: Letter stamps, square tags, and metal letters (Making Memories); rub-on letters (Autumn Leaves); green and olive cardstocks; acrylic paint; square brads; ribbon; string; black stamping ink; foam tape

A Gentle Side

Lee was delighted to capture a gentler side of her rough-and-tumble son as he gingerly supported three delicate butterflies on his fingertips. Ribbon charms serve as clever tabs for additional pull-out photographs.

Lee Zwicker, Victoria, British Columbia, Canada

Supplies: Patterned paper (Me & My Big Ideas); vellum tags, rub-on words and ribbon charms (Making Memories); printed metal disc (K & Company); label holder (Magic Scraps); tan and red cardstocks; brads; eyelet; circle punches; ribbon; vellum; acrylic paint; cord; green stamping ink

I is for Ice

ice (is) n. frozen water, made by cold

Snow Princess

A pink monochromatic layout matches the winter coat, hat (and nose) of Libby's daughter. Libby painted stencil letters with acrylic paint for her snowy title and used a sticker to finish it off.

Libby Weifenbach, Van Buren, Arkansas

Supplies: Patterned papers (Mustard Moon); stickers and preprinted vellum (Memories Complete); date stamp (Making Memories); letter stencils; acrylic paint; black stamping ink

Lunta Lunta Talvella (Snow Snow in the Winter)

There was so much hard-packed snow one January that Susanna's daughter could practically walk right into her favorite climbing tree. Susanna placed metal snowflake charms behind watch crystals for simple embellishments.

Susanna Tunturi-Anttila, Helsinki, Finland

Supplies: Patterned papers (Chatterbox, Paper Company); metal letters, metal washer words and snowflake charms (Making Memories); letter stickers (EK Success, Wordsworth); watch crystals; fibers; wood veneer tag; thread; corner slot punch

Snow Day

April designed a frigid-looking layout to match wintry black-and-white photos. She splattered the backs of printed transparencies with acrylic paint to give them a dusting of snow, then painted, embossed, then sanded metal letter tags until they looked frosty.

April Kleinfeldt, Greensboro, North Carolina

Supplies: Patterned paper (Colorbök); metal letter tags and metal plaque (Making Memories); snowflake charms (www.twopeasinabucket.com); slate blue, ice blue and white cardstocks; fibers; transparency; safety pins; eyelets; acrylic paints; embossing powder; thread

Uncharted Territory

A fresh snowfall can transform a town into a winter wonderland, as Martha documents. Martha wanted her photos alone to tell the story of this wintry day, so she kept her embellishments to a single collaged tag and a few well-chosen words.

Martha Crowther, Salem, New Hampshire

Supplies: Rub-on words (Making Memories); snowflake stamp (Magenta); peace tag (Target); patterned paper (source unknown); red and black cardstocks; fibers; ribbon; plastic snowflake charms; decorative button; paint chips; tag

We Love Snow

Two bundled-up girls and a snowy backdrop are the perfect combination for a classic black-and-white portrait. Wine charms hung from small die-cut frames create a quick and easy border.

Lisa Francis, New Castle, Indiana

Supplies: Embossed paper (Jennifer Collection); die-cut frames (Leeco); snowflake charms (Making Memories); white cardstock; wine glass charms; black pen

Winter Colors

Kathi's daughter Rebecca is one child that will never get lost in the snow in this jacket! The coat reminded Kathi of Rebecca's bubbly personality and inspired her to try these wild papers on an atypical wintertime page.

Kathi Rerek, Scotch Plains, New Jersey

Supplies: Patterned papers (KI Memories); snowflake punches (Emagination Crafts); title letters and tags (QuickKutz); iridescent pigment powder (Ranger); hot pink and white cardstocks; eyelets; ribbon

Sled Wax

Vanessa's daughter was not happy about stopping play to pose for a winter's day photo, as her expression attests. A bright red snowflake coordinates with her daughter's jacket, ribbon and vintage accents.

Vanessa Spady, Virginia Beach, Virginia

Supplies: Patterned paper (Karen Foster Design); vintage stickers (Melissa Frances); brick, red, white cardstocks; ribbon; snowflake die cuts; black stamping ink; black pen

Winter Means...

Sande loves to be the first one out after a snowstorm when the snow is still pristine. This photo is a result of one of those magic moments. A random arrangement of cardstock and patterned paper strips pep up the photo mat. Faux stitching, created by rolling a seamstress' serrating wheel along the edges of the page, adds a subtle hint of texture.

Sande Krieger, Salt Lake City, Utah

Supplies: Patterned paper (Scenic Route Paper Co.); rub-on words (Making Memories); snowflakes (EK Success); red and black cardstocks; ribbon; tags

Vision

A quiet afternoon away from the holiday madness, some snow-covered branches, a camera and a camcorder can create artistic magic. Mesh paper adds a natural element and draws attention to Rebekah's detail photo.

Rebekah Dahlem, Rochester, Michigan

Supplies: Mesh paper (Magenta); tan cardstock; square punch

Winter Magic

Sparkling cardstock was the natural background choice for a layout about the magic of wintertime. A bit of embossing powder and clear glaze add icy touches to two types of metal title letters.

Jill Tennyson, Lafayette, Colorado

Supplies: Sparkle cardstock (National Cardstock); metal letters (Making Memories); clear glaze (Stampin' Up!); preprinted vellum; fibers; brads; embossing powder; embossing ink

Reminisce

Spring and winter views of the same rhododendron serve as a reminder that things can be beautiful in all seasons. A tea-dyed tag anchors collage elements that inspire thoughts of seasons gone by.

Susanna Tunturi-Anttila, Helsinki, Finland

Supplies: Patterned papers (Colorbök, KI Memories, 7 Gypsies); definition sticker and rectangle tag (Making Memories); epoxy sticker (Creative Imaginations); clock stamp (Rubber Stampede); letter tiles (source unknown); gray cardstock; fibers; tag; postage stamp; old painting ephemera; paper clip; mulberry paper ribbon; chalk

Snow Dog

This flake-sprinkled pup attests to the fact that humans aren't the only ones who love a good romp in the snow. Carey typed journaling on her computer, changed the fonts and colors on selected words and printed it on photo paper for a picture-perfect journaling block.

Carey Johnson, St. Cloud, Minnesota

Supplies: Die-cut words (source unknown); black and white cardstocks; ribbon

Brrr

Bundled children with frozen noses and chilly cheeks make fabulous scrapbooking subjects, as this page attests. To add to the cold feeling of these photos, April added "fog" and "ice" with image-editing software and designed letters that look like they were carved from ice.

April Anderton, Post Falls, Idaho

Supplies: Image-editing software (Adobe Photoshop); brads and paper strip images (www.digitalscrapbooking.com)

Snow Day Fun!

A splash of patterned paper, a stamped photo mat and a smiling daughter are all you need for a vibrant winter page. Amy added a few embroidery floss stitches to secure title words and background cardstock.

Amy Goldstein, Kent Lakes, New York

Supplies: Patterned papers (American Crafts, Rusty Pickle); snowflake charms, rub-on word and label holder (Making Memories); photo clips (7 Gypsies); letter stickers (SEI); letter stamps (Hero Arts); orange cardstock; fibers; brown stamping ink

How to Make a Snow Angel

Ann had photos of her son with a look of trepidation, crying and laughing as he made his first snow angel, so she scrapbooked it all with a sense of humor. Using image-editing software, she added drop shadows to the numbers to give them a three-dimensional look.

Ann Hetzel Gunkel, Chicago, Illinois
Photos: David J. Gunkel, Chicago, Illinois

Supplies: Image-editing software (Adobe Photoshop); clip art (www.havanastreet.com)

J is for Journey

jour•ney (jur´ne) n. the act or an instance of traveling from one place to another

Youth

Melissa saw a commercial for a bedding set with diagonal lines which inspired this background design. She cut cardstocks and patterned paper in diagonal strips and used ribbon and brads to adhere a transparency over all elements.

Melissa Chapman, Regina, Saskatchewan, Canada

Supplies: Patterned paper, letter stamps and metal letters (Making Memories); preprinted transparency (Memories Complete); pink, salmon, brown, burgundy and white cardstocks; brads; ribbon; tags; button; brown stamping ink; extra thick embossing powder

Where Will Those Little Feet...

In his early days of walking, Christine muses over where her son's feet will take him. She created a small belt embellishment by adding eyelets and a buckle to walnut ink-dyed canvas tape.

Christine Drumheller, Zeeland, Michigan

Supplies: Patterned papers (Club Scrap); buckle (Rusty Pickle); label holder and metal letters (Making Memories); sticker (EK Success); black, red and cream cardstocks; eyelets, canvas tape; bead chain; tags; date stamp; brads; walnut ink; black stamping ink

Look Beyond...

This is the last page in an album Pam created for her 18-year-old sister's graduation—meant to inspire her for the future. The juxtaposition of irregular, "messy" word strips and clean, precise label tape makes for an effective and compelling title treatment.

Pam Rawn, Champlin, Minnesota

Supplies: Preprinted ribbon, word washer, eyelet plaque and rub-on words (Making Memories); letter stamps (Hero Arts); typewriter key (7 Gypsies); epoxy word sticker (Creative Imaginations); pine needle stamp (Stampin' Up!); red, green and sage cardstocks; label tape; brads; ribbon; watch crystal; letter beads; safety pin; charm; mesh; fibers; black stamping ink

Journey

A dramatic page illustrates that sometimes the journey is much more valuable and important than the destination. Amy stamped title letters on brick red cardstock, then cut each out to ensure the letters would stand out against the gray background.

Amy Stultz, Mooresville, Indiana

Supplies: Patterned paper (Tumblebeasts); label sticker (Pebbles); buckle (www.maudeandmillie.com); letter stamps (Ma Vinci's Reliquary); label maker (Dymo); photo corners (Canson); black and brick cardstocks; ribbon; black stamping ink

Together

This page celebrates the idea that people can depend on others and do not have to travel through life alone. Mary tore a piece of map patterned paper and cut small squares from it to complement her page theme.

Mary Faith Roell, Harrison, Ohio

Supplies: Patterned paper (7 Gypsies); mesh (Magic Mesh); word charms (source unknown); pumpkin, brick and red cardstocks; embroidery floss

The Journey...

This darling photo, complete with stuffed hankie tied to a stick, is a classic illustration for Jackie's title. For the word "step," Jackie layered two different types of stickers to achieve a shadowed effect.

Jackie Pettit, Morgan, Utah

Supplies: Patterned paper and printed vellum (Chatterbox); letter stickers (Creative Imaginations, Mrs. Grossman's); green and black cardstocks; photo corners; fibers; charm

TIME

Time

This page is part of an album Jackie created for her son to house inspirational quotes. She sprayed vellum with stone paint to create realistic-looking sand for her hourglass.

Jackie Siperko, Dallas, Pennsylvania

Supplies: Spray paint (Plasti-Kote); charm (source unknown); white and black cardstocks; acrylic paints; vellum; raffia

Be patient enough to live one day at a time, let yesterday go and leave tomorrow until it arrives.

Longitude: Whatever

Sam found her title phrase in a Florida vacation guide and thought it perfectly expressed the mood of this carefree vacation photo. She printed the title on a transparency that covers the entire layout. Bamboo clips attached to fibers lend exotic flavor.

Sam Cousins, Trumbull, Connecticut

Supplies: Patterned paper (Wübie); bamboo clips (7 Gypsies); white cardstock; transparency; fibers

K is for Kites

kite (kite) n. a light frame, covered, and to be flown at the end of a string in a light breeze

Breezy Days

Sheila documented a bonding moment between her son and his uncle on a breezy kite-flying day. She layered mesh and cardstock in several different arrangements for her border squares, embossed them with clear powder and added circle clips to tie in with her metal title letters.

Sheila Boehmert, Island Lake, Illinois

Supplies: Large weave netting (Magenta); metal letters and circle clips (Making Memories); mesh (Magic Mesh); blue cardstocks; extra thick embossing powder

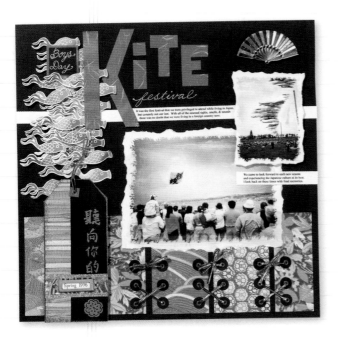

Boys Day Kite Festival

A kite festival in Japan warrants a page with distinct Asian flair. Samantha stamped fish on white cardstock using a multicolored ink pad, cut them out and layered them in a group with foam tape.

Samantha Walker, Battle Ground, Washington

Supplies: Washi and grass papers (FLAX art and design); label holder (Making Memories); fish kite and kanji stamps (Stampin' Up!); flower stamp (All Night Media); fan charm (Magic Scraps); black and white cardstocks; date stamp; label holder; eyelets; gold cord; gold leafing pen; embossing powder; colored stamping inks; foam tape

Flyin' High

Forget the playground...let's watch Daddy fly his really cool kite! Sherri emphasized the word "fun" in her journaling by printing it on lighter colored cardstock and mounting it with foam tape. She wove silver thread around her title letters to give the feeling of a tangled kite line.

Sherri Little, Southlake, Texas

Supplies: Patterned paper (Current); patterned vellum (Westrim); letter template (Provo Craft); metallic thread (Kreinik); washer eyelets (Creative Impressions); triangle eyelets (Happy Hammer); light blue, blue, navy and red cardstocks; metal-rimmed tags; circle clips; hole punch; tags; fibers; eyelets; beads; foam tape

Dream

The casual observer sees a boy holding tight to his kite string, which Jackie relates to holding tight to one's dreams as seen in her page design. A sticker border with words was used to separate the top and bottom halves of the page.

Jackie Siperko, Dallas, Pennsylvania

Supplies: Patterned papers (Daisy D's, Pebbles); stickers (Pebbles); rub-on words (Making Memories); tan cardstock

Go Fly a Kite

When Mom is busy caring for newborn twins, what is a boy to do on a windy day but make his own kite with notebook paper and staples? To create the word "kite," Michelle printed and cut out letters and pressed them gently into clay (rolled flat). She then cut the letters from clay, let them dry, applied paint and sealed them with decoupage glue for a shiny finish.

Michelle Pendleton, Colorado Springs, Colorado

Supplies: Clay (Creative Paperclay); letter stamps (Hero Arts); rub-on words (Creative Imaginations, Making Memories); star brads (Creative Impressions); green, brown, tan and speckled cardstocks; acrylic paint; chalk; twine; embroidery floss; decoupage glue; brown stamping ink

Spring Fever

A dose of spring fever makes kids a little bit like kites, according to Kelli—they get stuck in trees, roll in the breezes and forget what time to come home. A broad band of solid color along the bottom of her focal-point photo was the perfect spot for a rub-on title.

Kelli Noto, Centennial, Colorado

Supplies: Rub-on words (Making Memories); rub-on date (Creative Imaginations); white cardstock

L is for Leaves

leaf (leef) n. any of the flat expanded organs, usually green, growing laterally from the stem or twig of a plant

A Season of Change

Many people have classic shots of children in the colorful fall foliage, but Krista enhanced this spread with photos of other fall sights—fallen leaves, a pile of pumpkins and ripe watermelons. She tried to emulate the dried, aged look of the leaves by coloring her definition stickers with different inks.

Krista Goodwin, Indianapolis, Indiana

Supplies: Patterned paper and die-cut frame (Chatterbox); rub-on words and definition stickers (Making Memories); stickers (Creative Imaginations, EK Success); yellow, brick and green cardstocks; eyelets; walnut ink; green and orange stamping inks

Autumn Magic

Bernie converted her photo to black-and-white and let her design choices provide the colors. She added richness to her design by using suede paper beneath gold leaf buttons and outlining her journaling block with gold beads.

Bernie Silvan, Drexel Hill, Pennsylvania

Supplies: Patterned paper (EK Success); suede paper (Hot Off The Press); leaf buttons (Jesse James); metallic gold and pumpkin cardstocks; beads; vellum

Autumn Day

Andrea captured an autumn day spent in the botanic gardens collecting leaves for a school project. She created custom leaf embellishments by rolling out the clay, pressing real leaves into it, brushing them with metallic pigment powder, trimming out each one and baking them to harden.

Andrea Manard, Memphis, Tennessee

Supplies: Patterned paper (Print Blocks); pigment powder (Jacquard Products); letter stamps (Wordsworth); metal letters (Making Memories); pumpkin and green cardstocks; mulberry paper; polymer clay; eyelets; fibers; embossing ink; embossing powder

Season of Youth

Various accents with an autumn feel frame this photo of Robin's children sitting in a pile of leaves. For her title, she held bright copper letter brads over an open flame to change their color. Leaf images stamped with watermark ink provide subtle embellishments.

Robin Bell, Calgary, Alberta, Canada

Supplies: Patterned papers and letter brads (Provo Craft); leaf stamps (Stampin' Up!); wire ornaments (Too Funky); gold, burgundy, tan and brown cardstocks; square brads; chalk; metallic rub-ons; foam tape; brown, purple and watermark stamping inks

Autumn's Splendor

A flurry of close-cropped photos allowed Michelle to capture many aspects of fall on one page. She tore, rolled and chalked the edges of patterned paper for a textured background and machine-stitched her photo mat.

Michelle Hubbartt, Grand Junction, Colorado

Supplies: Patterned paper (Karen Foster Design); vellum tags (EK Success); leaf embellishments (Boutique Trims); orange, rust and green cardstocks; fibers; thread; eyelets; vellum; chalk; brown pen

The Ups and Downs of Autumn

Anne captured all her favorite aspects of autumn in two charming minibooks, tabbed for easy access and filled with photos and journaling. For her title, she painted wooden tiles with acrylic paint and pigment powder, then added letter stickers darkened with a pen.

Anne Heyen, New Fairfield, Connecticut

Supplies: Pigment powder (Jacquard Products); rivets (Chatterbox); gold leafing pen (Krylon); oval punch (Emagination Crafts); gum arabic (Winsor Newton); gold, tan and brown cardstocks; brads; wooden tiles; acrylic paint; vellum; embossing powder; brown stamping ink

First Signs of Fall

Rhonda's family decided to celebrate the onset of fall with a walk in an arboretum...that is, until Grandma tired out! The title was traced from a lettering template, covered with pieces of mesh and stitched with different colors of embroidery floss.

Rhonda Pflugh, Canton, Ohio

Supplies: Patterned paper (Bo-Bunny Press, Design Originals); letter template (Scrap Pagerz); letter stamps (Hero Arts); definition stickers (Making Memories); 3-D fall stickers (EK Success); tan, rust, green and taupe cardstocks; mesh; brads; embroidery floss; brown stamping ink

Fall

Amber documented her sons' feelings about fall in these personality-filled photographs and included journaling straight from their mouths. To make her background design, she traced leaf die cuts, stitched the outlines with embroidery floss and chalked inside the stitching.

Amber Baley, Waupun, Wisconsin

Supplies: Patterned papers (Provo Craft); vellum; eyelets; embroidery floss; chalk; hinges

1

L is for Love

love (luv) n. 1 a deep and tender affection, attachment or devotion to a person or persons

True Love

Sue's grandchildren are the "ABCs"—Aubrey, Braiden and Camden, so when she saw them sitting in exactly the right order, she couldn't help but snap a photo and record how much they rock her world. She used photo anchors as a pull tab for her journaling pocket and further decorated the pocket with ribbon, metal accents, a safety pin and preprinted twill.

Sue Fields, South Whitley, Indiana

Supplies: Preprinted transparency and "stitched" epoxy border stickers (K & Company); library pocket and card (Autumn Leaves); preprinted twill (All My Memories); ribbon charm, word washer, jump ring, photo anchors and zipper pulls (Making Memories); cream, black and olive cardstocks; acrylic paint; ribbon; safety pin; brad; foam tape

Embrace

Two sisters who love to snuggle with one another is truly something to celebrate. Various aged definition stickers come together to make a fun collaged accent, and a weathered tag draws attention to the word "embrace."

Danielle Toews, East Falmouth, Massachusetts

Supplies: Patterned paper (Chatterbox); definition and word stickers (Pebbles); heart clip (Making Memories); red cardstock; ribbon; safety pin; black stamping ink

To Be Young and Beautiful

Suzanne's son and his date were good sports posing for her mini photo shoot before the prom. Suzanne used a plastic label holder as a unique pull tab for hidden journaling. White rub-on letters stand out nicely on a black embossed background.

Suzanne Webb, Redmond, Oregon

Supplies: Patterned papers (7 Gypsies, KI Memories); preprinted accent (KI Memories); letter rub-ons (Making Memories); label holder (Sweetwater); yellow and black cardstocks; photo corners; ribbon

Now and Forever

A tender kiss between two people in love is the focus of this layout. Angela adorned a metal heart with a bit of red paper yarn, then placed it inside a slide mount to coordinate with the other hearts on the layout.

Angela Green, Georgetown, Illinois

Supplies: Patterned paper (Paper Company); printed twill (7 Gypsies); heart clip, metal heart, paper yarn and rub-on words (Making Memories); black and white cardstocks; date stamp; slide mount; metal frame; black stamping ink

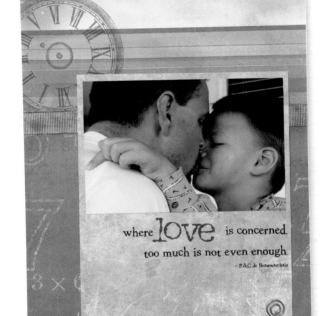

Where Love Is Concerned...

This simple page celebrates that relationship between a father and son with loving elegance. Changing the photo to black-and-white creates an element of tenderness and ensures that it stands out against background patterns.

Layle Koncar, Sandy, Utah

Supplies: Patterned papers (7 Gypsies, Karen Foster Design); clock face stamp (Magenta); letter stamps (Stampers Anonymous); "s" clip (Making Memories); brown stamping ink

Big Brothers Are Hugs From God

Jill's title on this layout says it all, especially from the perspective of a little sister. Jill painted metal words with white and green paint, then lightly rubbed some of the green off to give them a mottled appearance.

Jill J. Mills, Roswell, Georgia

Supplies: Patterned papers (Rusty Pickle); letter stamps, metal words and ribbon charm (Making Memories); preprinted transparency (source unknown); green and black cardstocks; paint chip; letter beads; brads; ribbon; acrylic paints

Kissing Cousins

Little did Jennifer know that when she asked her son to sit next to his cousin for a quick photo, they would start kissing and hugging each other for the entire photo shoot. Coordinating stickers make for a quick and easy layout.

Jennifer Keastead, Highland Lakes, New Jersey

Supplies: Stickers (Pebbles); heart clips (Making Memories); letter stickers (Creative Imaginations); red, green and tan cardstocks; wire; letter beads; twine

Tower of Love

A tower of blocks and two toy people are an unconventional but sweet way to record a daughter's love for her dad. Alison transcribed the conversation between herself and her daughter verbatim as her daughter built the arrangement with "James and Daddy" on top.

Alison Chabe, Charlestown, Massachusetts

Supplies: Patterned paper (Deluxe Designs); embossed paper (source unknown); flower stamp (Hero Arts); rub-on letters and clip (Making Memories); pink and magenta cardstocks; rose and gray stamping inks

We Are Shaped...

Ten years of marriage is a perfect reason to celebrate someone who inspired you to become the person you wanted to be. Rachael created an almost-invisible flap for fold-out journaling from torn orange cardstock on the left side of her layout.

Rachael Giallongo, Auburn, New Hampshire

Supplies: Patterned paper (Creative Imaginations); tacks (Chatterbox); rub-on word and ribbon charm (Making Memories); photo corners (Canson); burgundy and orange cardstocks; ribbon

Our Love Story

This dramatic silhouette makes the perfect opening page for an album about a courtship. A simple bar of patterned papers and a bit of wire add an elegant accompaniment to Hanni's title page.

Hanni Baumgardner, Winona Lake, Indiana
Photo: Carissa Mikel, Etna Green, Indiana

Supplies: Patterned papers (Anna Griffin, K & Company); black and cream cardstocks; patterned papers; wire; eyelets; brads; black pen

So Sweet

Ten years may separate this brother and sister, but their hearts couldn't be closer. Rub-ons and suede paper stitched directly to the background make for a creative, textured title.

Sharon Laakkonen, Superior, Wisconsin

Supplies: Patterned and suede papers (K & Company); flower charms (www.twopeas inabucket.com); mesh ribbon (www.scrap muse.com); rub-on letters (Making Memories); green cardstock; embroidery floss; acrylic paint; red stamping ink

A Kiss

This playful photo really looks like J.J.'s friend was stopped in the midst of speech by a sweet, unexpected kiss. This page is a fun exploration of layers and depth, with some areas cut away to reveal patterns and embellishments underneath.

J.J. Killins, Redondo Beach, California

Supplies: Patterned papers (Jennifer Collection, K & Company, Pebbles, Provo Craft); preprinted vellum (DieCuts with a View); cream cardstock; vellum

Soulmates

Cindy cherishes seeing her sister so happy and in love, and this page reflects that one-of-a-kind relationship. A compelling photo, a few photo anchors, and some coordinating stickers pull this page together with elegance and beauty.

Cindy Johnson-Bentley, Allen, Texas

Supplies: Patterned papers (Karen Foster Design, Scrap Ease); stickers (Pebbles); photo anchors (Scrappy's); black and cream cardstocks

Wherever Life Takes Us...

This tender photo of a father comforting his baby son who is frightened of his swimming pool can serve as a photo study showing the contrast of big and small. Safety pins and machine stitching anchor the fabric photo mat and caption strip, keeping with the aged feel of the background paper.

Christine Drumheller, Zeeland, Michigan

Supplies: Patterned papers (Design Originals, K & Company); tag (7 Gypsies); stickers (EK Success); number stickers (K & Company); conchos (Coffee Break Design); brown cardstock; fabric; embroidery floss; safety pins; sewing machine; brown stamping ink

An Enduring Tenderness

The love between a mother and son is embraced through textured paper, flowing fibers and smooth preprinted accents. Mellette created this page to express how her son has always been a part of her, even before he was born.

Mellette Berezoski, Crosby, Texas

Supplies: Patterned paper (K & Company, Paper Company, Provo Craft); preprinted frame and rose tag (Leeco); epoxy sticker (Creative Imaginations); square brads (Magic Scraps); ribbon; large brad; black cardstock; fibers

Father

Using image-editing software, Dana transformed an assortment of color photos to black-and-white so they would coordinate with one another. The page cherishes the love between Carlie and her daddy while maintaining a masculine flavor with brown suede paper and an earth-toned color scheme.

Dana Swords, Doswell, Virginia

Supplies: Patterned paper (Colorbök); suede paper (K & Company); tag, heart corner and plate (Making Memories); color-blocking templates (Deluxe Designs); stamps (All Night Media); ribbon (Offray); dark green, light green and cream cardstocks; brown and black stamping ink; vellum; fibers

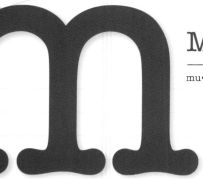

M is for Music

mu•sic (myoo´ zik) n. the art and science of combining vocal or instrumental sounds or tones

Music Lover

Independent blocks of color are music to the eyes on this page featuring Mellette's pint-size pianist. Various music-note patterned papers paired with ribbon, tags and letter buttons suit her theme and match her daughter's outfit.

Mellette Berezoski, Crosby, Texas

Supplies: Patterned papers (Amscan, Karen Foster Design, Mustard Moon, 7 Gypsies); ribbon (Making Memories); gold letter buttons (Nunn Design); round tag and small tag (DMD); music charm (Jest Charming); black cardstock; embossing powder; brads; embroidery floss; thread

At Your Fingertips Is...

The simplicity of a song is captured in this acoustic design, accented only through direct-to-paper inking and label maker tape. Becky keeps the focus of the page on the "music" coming from the guitar in the photo.

Becky Thompson, Fruitland, Idaho

Supplies: Patterned paper (Rusty Pickle); letter stickers (Creative Imaginations); stamps (Hero Arts); label maker (Dymo); mustard, black and brown cardstocks; black stamping ink

Make a Joyful Noise

Becky's page sings with a visual energy that celebrates her son's first preschool performance...and first case of stage fright. Layers of patterned papers and decorative fabric trim commemorate the moment on a high note.

Becky Kent, Hilliard, Ohio

Supplies: Brown textured cardstock (Bazzill); patterned papers (DieCuts with a View, K & Company, Li'l Davis Designs, Provo Craft); letter die cuts and small frame (QuicKutz); letter stickers (Sticker Studio); date stamp (Rogers); ribbon (source unknown); ephemera (Me & My Big Ideas); twill (Wrights); black cardstock; brads; button; fibers; staples; sewing machine

Music Is the Way...

A preprinted transparency over layers of patterned papers adds a lively and playful tune to Keri's collage-style page. Shimmering and metallic ribbons give this page pizazz.

Keri Key, Burlington, North Carolina

Supplies: Patterned papers (Penny Black); preprinted transparency (Creative Imaginations); die-cut frame (My Mind's Eye); ribbon (Offray); jewelry tags (Office Depot); heart charm (Card Connection); safety pin; walnut ink; brads

Music

To create harmony between the vintage-looking patterned paper and the metal embellishments, Shauna inked and sanded frames, photo corners, punch-outs and brads. She mounted both the photo and the layout itself on metallic gold paper which she inked for a brushed gold effect.

Shauna Berglund-Immel for Hot Off The Press, Beaverton, Oregon

Supplies: Patterned paper and metallic gold paper, vintage ephemera, buckle, frames, brads and corner punch-outs (Hot Off The Press); letter stamps (Hero Arts); black and white cardstocks; black stamping ink; foam tape; fine-grain sandpaper; hole punch; eyelet setter

Sweet Music

Soft and dreamy tones and textures create a visual lullaby on this page, showcasing Elizabeth's daughter and violin. Button accents serve as pegs for mini dangling tags stamped with the letter names of the violin strings.

Elizabeth Ruuska, Rensselaer, Indiana

Supplies: Button paper (K & Company); patterned paper (Rusty Pickle); textured paper (Bazzill); jewelry tags (www.twopeasinabucket.com); photo corners (Close To My Heart); letter stickers (Creative Imaginations); rub-on letters (Making Memories); antique letter stamps (PSX Design); black stamping ink; antique buttons; thread

Love Is Not Measured...

Elizabeth added tightly cropped detail shots of a violin on the left side of this spread that honors her husband for beginning his violin teacher training. Tags containing a quote balance the left and right sides, accompanied by a personal note written by Elizabeth.

Elizabeth Ruuska, Rensselaer, Indiana

Supplies: Patterned papers (Creative Imaginations, 7 Gypsies); tags and gold clock (7 Gypsies); printed vellum (Colorbök); handmade paper (source unknown); gold metallic cardstock (Club Scrap); letter stamps (Ma Vinci's Reliquary); metal ball chain (American Tag); metal label holder (source unknown); gold stamping ink; burnt orange cardstock; brads; square punch; circle punch; walnut ink

m

Practice Makes Perfect

Wanting to play with the theme of the brassy baritone, Dawn used an engraving tool to etch words onto a transparency, using brass letter templates as guides. A montage of letter charms and slide mounts provides a pleasingly playful title.

Dawn Burden, Franklin, Tennessee

Supplies: Patterned paper (K & Company); decorative transparency, letter stencils and engraving tool (Magic Scraps); slide mounts (Design Originals); letter charms, page pebbles, eyelets, jump rings (Making Memories); black hemp (Crafts Etc.); metal label holders (Li'l Davis Designs); ribbon; black stamping ink; mustard, red and black cardstocks; silver brads

Field Musicians

In order to re-enact a Civil War-era feeling across this spread of her son's field musician weekend, Judi used image-editing software to transform color photos to sepia. She then tore and chalked the photos' edges and creased them at various points to produce an aged look.

Judi Kirby, Newark, Ohio

Supplies: Patterned paper, patriotic stickers (Karen Foster Design); star eyelets (Making Memories); image-editing software (Adobe Photoshop); black, red, tan and black cardstocks; letter template; chalk; twine; fibers; corrugated paper; wire

The Heart of a Musician

Erika created a symphony of beauty on this page, using a collage of music note patterned papers, paints and embossing, all to accent the photo of Jade. She scratched the edges of the photo to meld with the distressed look of the page.

Erika Hayes, Phoenix, Arizona

Supplies: Patterned papers (Rusty Pickle, 7 Gypsies, USArtQuest); letter stamps, photo corners, tag, deco stamps, acrylic paint and washer word (Making Memories); "heart" stickers (EK Success); "of" rub-ons (Creative Imaginations); preprinted "A" (Foofala); letter stamps (Ma Vinci's Reliquary); "Ex-Libris" book identification card (source unknown); mica (USArtQuest); tag (American Tag); fibers; mini bag; embossing powder; cardstock; marker; brown stamping ink; brads

American Idol

Not only does this little star light up this page with her beaming bright eyes, but her voice takes center stage as well. Recorded on a Memory Button is Libby's daughter's rendition of Clay Aiken's "Invisible." Libby's pull-out journaling behind the photo shares her daughter's love for music and certain artists, including two stars from "American Idol."

Libby Weifenbach, Van Buren, Arkansas

Supplies: Patterned papers and perforated title letters (Mustard Moon); Memory Button (Ellison); arrow sticker (Sassafras Lass); heart/flag sticker (Pebbles); metal-rimmed tag (Making Memories); letter stickers (Sticker Studio); label maker (Dymo); "November" sticker (Creative Imaginations); letter stickers (Colorbök); black chalk stamping ink; gingham ribbon; black pen

Kendra has always loved singing. I'm sure it's because music is such an important part of our daily lives. When she went to Branson with her Grandma & Grandpa Weifenbach, I wasn't surprised to find her playing this new guitar. She was suddenly a performer! Her favorite singers are Shania Twain, Toby Keith, Rascal Flatts, and (from the American Idol TV show) Clay Aiken & Kimberley Locke. She knows many of their songs and isn't at all shy about belting them out. Push the button at the top of the page to hear her sing Clay Aiken's "Invisible."

I Let the Music Do the Talking

Nancy created this layout of memories or feelings evoked by her favorite CDs, which in turn reveals bits of her personality. She printed out reduced-sized images of CD labels from her own collection and altered her self-portrait with image-editing software for a unique look.

Nancy Trunzo, Shingle Springs, California

Supplies: Patterned paper (Paper Patch); printed transparency (www.MemoryMakinDivas.com); ribbons (Me & My Big Ideas); image-editing software (Paint Shop Pro by Jasc); red cardstock; chalk; black stamping ink

Christmas Recital

For Sande, it is the sounds of her sons tickling the ivories that make her season merry and bright, as is expressed inside a hidden journaling pocket. Stitching around page elements softens the design, keeping it masculine while adding homespun charm.

Sande Krieger, Salt Lake City, Utah

Supplies: Patterned papers (Artistic Scrapper, K & Company, 7 Gypsies); decorative brad (Making Memories); coins (EK Success); thread; postage stamp (K & Company); postage stamp scissors (Fiskars); black cardstock; sewing machine

Drummer Boy

Melanie designed this page to capture her brother's passion for drums. Sage paper brings black-and-white photos to life, and the repetition of circular shapes in the metal-rimmed tag, circle clip and paper punch add a rhythm all their own.

Melanie Gautreau
Fredericton, New Brunswick, Canada

Supplies: Patterned papers (7 Gypsies, Sweetwater); letter stickers (Sticker Studio, Wordsworth); metal-rimmed circle tag (Avery); date stamp (Office Depot); letter stamp (EK Success); safety pin (Making Memories); white cardstock; black and sage stamping inks; black string, black brads

Little Music Maker

When Teri's daughter used a flower arrangement for a music stand, it struck a chord with her to capture the moment. Acrylic paints, hidden journaling and distressing techniques provide an expressive backdrop for an 8 x 10" focal-point photo, while cropped photos tucked neatly in two corners highlight the details.

Teri Fode, Carmichael, California

Supplies: Patterned papers (Colorbök, Paper Loft, Rusty Pickle); metal mesh (Scrapyard 329); ribbon (Offray); photo anchors (Making Memories); letter stamps (Hero Arts, PSX Design); foam letter stamps (Duncan); treble-clef die cut (source unknown)

One afternoon I stumbled upon Tori practicing her clarinet with her music propped up in the floral arrangement instead of on her music stand. It made me smile because we were at Grandma Fode's house and she had forgotten to bring the stand. Innovatively, she saw the perfect prop! She was determined to get her practice session in no matter what...she is very dedicated to keeping her commitment to her music studies.

MAR 2004

N is for Nature

na•ture (na´ cher) n. the power, force, principle, etc, that seems to regulate the physical universe

Lazy Days

A peaceful day by the riverbank rolls across this page with soothing tones and textures. Tammy stitched handmade paper into a fold-out element that reveals journaling about a new generation of memories on this bridge, where she once played as a child.

Tammy Young, St. Peters, Missouri

Supplies: Patterned papers and eyelets (Making Memories); white handmade title paper (DMD); dark and light green cardstocks; handmade journaling papers; vellum; fibers; chalk; jute

Forces of Nature

Shandy kept her design simple to allow the power of an enlarged photo to speak for itself. The deep purple cardstocks and black inked edges carry the ominous tones of stormy skies across the page, while a smaller cropped image in the lower right corner provides an added jolt of awe.

Shandy Vogt, Nampa, Idaho

Supplies: Letter stamps (Hero Arts); date stamp (Office Max); black stamping ink; black and purple cardstocks

Imagine Nature

Maegan followed her son's example of finding fascination in the simple things by photographing him as he closely examined ants. She inked the ends of wooden sticks and wrapped them with fibers for embellishment.

Maegan Hall, Virginia Beach, Virginia

Supplies: Patterned paper, stickers and border (Pebbles); jute, ribbon and sticks (Scrapfindings); sticker buttons (Karen Foster Design); fibers; brown and dark green cardstocks; black stamping ink; sand paper

Yellowstone

Fragments from an actual Yellowstone National Park map highlight Samantha's favorite drives and sights. A hand-bound book houses more photographs and journaling, with an old watch buckle and a paper strip wrapping around the outside for a leather-strap effect.

Samantha Walker
Battle Ground, Washington

Supplies: Fabric (Carole Fabrics); small light green and brown circle tags, yarn fibers, brads and inks (Stampin' Up!); eyelets (Making Memories); liquid gold pen (Marvy); metal label holder (Jo-Ann Fabrics); dark green, light green, dark brown and light brown cardstocks; watch buckle; narrow jute; Yellowstone map; antique printer stamps; sewing machine

Rainbow Connection

An enlarged photo of a rainbow serves as the background for this page as well as the foundation for journaling and a title. Shannon made two slices above and below her title in order to slip a piece of ribbon through. From the ribbon hangs colored tags with coordinating jump rings to represent each rainbow color.

Shannon Taylor, Bristol, Tennessee

Supplies: Ribbon (Offray); colored jump rings (Junkitz); gold brad (Doodlebug Design); black cardstock; foam tape; decorative chalks; square punch

The Hike

Jane re-created the feel of this day in the woods with several patterned papers, fibers and leaf accents that shout with the voice of the great outdoors. Her strand of coppery fibers seems to tie in with the photo of a snake seen on the hike.

Jane Swanson, Janesville, Wisconsin

Supplies: Dark brown speckled cardstock, green skeleton leaves and vellum (Club Scrap); patterned papers (EK Success, Two X Two Designs); fibers (Fibers By The Yard); leaf buttons (Jesse James); letter stickers (All My Memories); letter template (Wordsworth); brads; chalk; black pen

South Carolina Botanical Gardens

The beauty of nature is accented by silk flowers on April's page. A clock-face embellishment placed over ribbon signifies a memory captured in time.

April Kleinfeldt, Greensboro, North Carolina

Supplies: Patterned paper (Anna Griffin); mesh (Magenta); flowers (Michaels); ribbon (Offray); library card holder (Boxer Scrapbook Productions); stamp (source unknown); vintage watch face; transparency; safety pin; sage and brick cardstocks; gold photo corners; brown stamping ink

Journey

A great way to use up many photos on a page and provide an interactive adventure is to create mini books and fold-outs, as Julie incorporated on this layout. She scored 3 x 3" squares for the Journey book in the upper left corner, which is perfect for showcasing small or cropped photos. Each fold-out is fastened closed in a different way for added interest.

Julie Johnson, Seabrook, Texas

Supplies: Patterned paper (Karen Foster Design); metal letters, metal-rimmed square tags and definition stickers (Making Memories); pointing finger stamp (source unknown); stickers (Creative Imaginations, EK Success); clasp and walnut ink (7 Gypsies); dark and light brown and cream cardstocks; fibers; metal ball chain and toggle

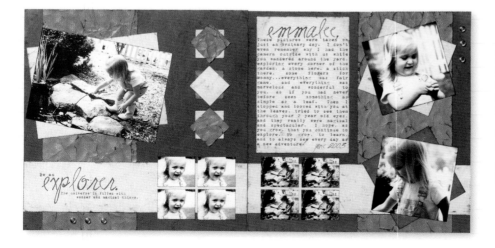

Explorer

Heather crumpled and inked her papers for textural visual terrain, capturing the zest of uncharted territory in her daughter's outdoor adventures. The images repeated in the lower right corner add a sense of movement and joy.

Heather D. White, Riverton, Utah
Photos: Michelle Ballard, Hagerstown, Maryland

Supplies: Patterned papers (Paper Patch); gold brads (Making Memories); black stamping ink; square punch

One Touch of Nature...

After illuminating her computer-generated page with rays of light for an awe-inspiring effect, Mikki scanned a metal clasp for faux three-dimensional charm. An appropriate quote serves as her title.

Mikki Livanos, Jacksonville, Florida

Supplies: Image-editing software (Adobe Photoshop and Illustrator); metal clasp (Darice)

It's the Simple Things of Life...

The emerald majesty of nature reigns on this page, surrounded by preprinted transparency accents. After accidentally spilling water on the left-side of the page, Lori sanded the paper to help it blend in. She liked the look so well, she sanded the edges of the photo too.

Lori Springer, Elkhart, Indiana

Supplies: Dark green paper and overlay (Memories Complete); preprinted transparencies (www.theembellishmentstore.com); definitions, letter, date stamps and pewter mini brads (Making Memories); photo turns (7 Gypsies); leaf charm (A Charming Place); light green cardstock

Green River

Angela created this two-page spread as part of a hometown series. With all the photos she had from her home in Wyoming, she thought this would be a good way to highlight the National Wildlife Refuge there and inspire others to take a second look at their own hometowns, states or country.

Angela M. Cable, Rock Springs, Wyoming

Supplies: Image-editing software (Paint Shop Pro by Jasc); background pattern, initial and feather clip art (Dover Publications)

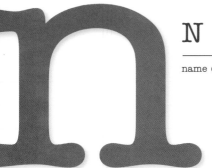

N is for Name

name (nam) n. a word or phrase by which a person, thing or class of things is known

Delaney

Lisa printed a list of Delaney's loves at age 8 on a transparency, using a font that looks like label maker tape. She attached the transparency with a silver hinge and added a metal tag with a bow in Delaney's favorite color.

Lisa Francis, New Castle, Indiana

Supplies: Patterned paper (PSX Design); letter stickers (Paper Loft); metal letter nailheads (Jo-Ann Fabrics); photo corners (Canson); hinge (source unknown); metal tag (source unknown); transparency; purple stamping ink; ribbon

Stephen

This priceless photo of her son was enough for Alison to keep the page focused on Stephen's impish grin, highlighting with a few fibers and handcut title. The heartfelt poem captured the ways Alison and her son complement each other to make a perfect whole.

Alison Penstone, Bracknell, Berkshire, England

Supplies: Patterned paper (Wordsworth); fibers, buttons and brads (Making Memories); vellum; embroidery floss; eyelets; cardstock; poem (www.twopeasinabucket.com)

Stella

The many expressions of Stella on this layout capture the heart of a mother's love. Alecia used letter stencils to create the title and accented them with charms and fibers. Love notes from Mommy are hidden beneath the focal-point photo.

Alecia Grimm, Atlanta, Georgia

Supplies: Patterned papers (Anna Griffin, Colorbök, Hot Off The Press); letter stencils (Target); flower brads (Making Memories); hinge (Home Depot); preprinted transparency (source unknown); letter stickers (EK Success); slide mount; gold paper clip; acrylic paint; pipe cleaner; charms; black pen; fabric; burnt sienna stamping ink; sage and pink cardstocks

Boy Crazy Brooke

Patricia made this page to highlight the favorite topic of her preteen niece Brooke, using Brooke's own quotes about boys. Patricia painted the photo itself with acrylic paint, adding rub-on letters over the paint once it dried.

Patricia Anderson, Selah, Washington

Supplies: Patterned papers, letter stamps, rub-on letters and letter charms (Making Memories); brown rivets (Doodlebug Design); paper letters (Mustard Moon); metal letter "B" (Pressed Petals); cream and brown textured cardstocks; ribbon; acrylic paint; sewing machine

Katie

Having two boys of her own, it tickled LeAnn to create this sweet pastel girly page of her friend's daughter. She stamped Katie's name with foam stamps in a pretty periwinkle, which coordinated with her pastel patterned background.

LeAnn Fane, Powder Springs, Georgia

Supplies: Patterned paper and metal word charm (K & Company); foam stamps, metal-rimmed tag and paint (Making Memories); number stamp, vellum, and ink (Stampin' Up!); fibers (Fibers By The Yard); epoxy heart sticker (Creative Imaginations); olive, light blue and periwinkle cardstocks; eyelet; rivets

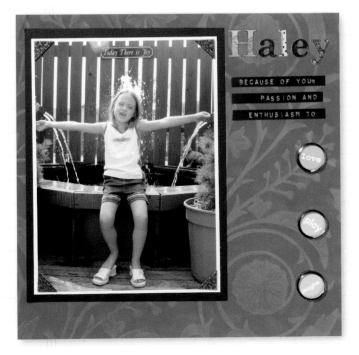

Haley

The sign on the fence in this photo said it all, so Lisa expanded on the phrase for her page title. She included joyful words in simple conchos for embellishment over an embossed velvet background.

Lisa Francis, New Castle, Indiana

Supplies: Teal velvet embossed paper (K & Company); conchos (Scrapworks); letter stickers (Creative Imaginations); label maker (Dymo); photo corners (Making Memories); black and white cardstocks

Tyler

Miki uses letters in Tyler's name to spell out his beloved qualities. The metal letter tags contrast against the blue paper to highlight his name amongst simple black letter stickers.

Miki Benedict, Modesto, California

Supplies: Lime green and aqua papers (Karen Foster Design); letter tags, buttons and eyelets (Making Memories); letter stickers (EK Success); twine

Jackson

The definition of Jackson's name, "God has shown favor," is given appropriate emphasis in Mary Anne's design. To create the vertical title block on the left side of the page, Mary Anne created a text box on her computer using a large, chunky font. She then created a separate text box, larger than the first, filled with the repeated name in white. By moving the white words over the chunky name and then removing the text box line, she created this name-in-name effect.

Mary Anne Walters, Ramsdell, Hampshire, England

Supplies: Computer-generated patterned paper (AppleWorks by Apple); letter punches (Letterman); metal letters tiles, metal letter circle tags and eyelets (Making Memories); letter beads (Westrim); letter stamps (PSX Design); black stamping ink; dark blue and black cardstocks

James

This soft and serious page uses muted tones to reflect the heart of a boy beyond his years, as Kenna suggests with a clock embellishment. To draw attention to her son's name, Kenna tore a hole from patterned paper, painted the edges and placed colored mesh and more patterned paper behind it. Painted metal letters were placed over the mesh.

Kenna Ewing, Parkside, Pennsylvania

Supplies: Patterned papers (Karen Foster Design, Pebbles, 7 Gypsies); letter stickers (Creative Imaginations); mesh and watch parts (Jest Charming); metal letter tiles (Making Memories); burgundy cardstock; black stamping ink

Alexander

This spirit-filled design is the result of a scanned and printed dictionary page, on which the theme word was highlighted with a green pen. Jlyne used simple strips of green cardstock to mat her journaling and photo.

Jlyne Hanback, Biloxi, Mississippi

Supplies: Square metal-rimmed vellum tag and green eyelet (Making Memories); sticker (Creative Imaginations); green and white cardstocks; dictionary

Cherish Sarah

The heart of Elizabeth's layout is Sarah, which is evidenced by a metal heart accent covered with white extra thick embossing powder. She also stamped the title with embossing ink and applied the same embossing powder over the letters.

Elizabeth Cuzzacrea, Lockport, New York

Supplies: Patterned papers (Chatterbox, Pebbles); stickers and letters (Pebbles); metal heart and door knocker (www. maudeandmillie.com); ribbon and brad (Making Memories); large letter stamps (Ma Vinci's Reliquary); word sticker (Creative Imaginations); olive cardstock; black pen; black stamping and embossing inks; white extra thick embossing powder

Bernie

Wanting to create a page that was beautifully Bernie, Carolyn tried to use all the colors of this sweet pooch's fur in her accents and letters. A variety of letter stickers showcase the dog's name.

Carolyn Cleveland, Maysville, Georgia

Supplies: Patterned papers and brown, dark brown and cream cardstocks (Club Scrap); corrugated paper (DMD); farm letter die cuts and metal letter brads (Carolee's Creations); stickers (Bo-Bunny Press, Creative Imaginations, EK Success, Magenta, Paper Loft); flower brad (Making Memories)

Ben

For a unique photo treatment, Sam made two copies of Ben's photo—one color and one black-and-white. She then tore the face section from the color copy and placed it over the black-and-white copy. She inked the tiles, twill and tag edges for a look that is all boy...and all Ben.

Sam Cousins, Trumbull, Connecticut

Supplies: Patterned paper, transparency, sticker and tiles (Sweetwater); decorative brad (Making Memories); twill tape; sepia ink; fibers; date stamp

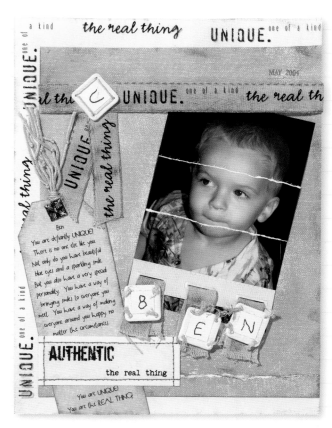

Jasper

Elizabeth dedicated this canine creation to the many aliases of her four-legged friend. After spelling out Jasper's name on a transparency, she brushed white acrylic paint across the back as well as on the photo itself.

Elizabeth Cuzzacrea, Lockport, New York

Supplies: Patterned paper (Anna Griffin); letter stickers (Chatterbox, Creative Imaginations, Doodlebug Design, EK Success); label maker (Dymo); ribbon (Wal-Mart); metal mesh and purple staples (Making Memories); purple, tan and light green cardstocks; transparency; black stamping ink; acrylic paint

Trust Me...

Sarah used tons of textures and embellishments of all things green and alive on this spread of James, bringing out his mischievous nature. She printed her journaling onto canvas, stitching it in place on the right-hand page.

Sarah Moore, Canberra, Australian Capital Territory, Australia

Supplies: Patterned paper, words and numbers (Creative Imaginations); dark green textured paper (Carolee's Creations); clay (Creative Paperclay Company); letter buttons (Junkitz); clear letter charms, white metal label holder, metal letters and numbers (Making Memories); pewter leaf stickers (Magenta); definition paper (source unknown); light and dark green cardstocks; thread; canvas material; eyelets; string; twig

Google Me

Alison was thrilled when a list of "googleisms" surfaced from www.google.com when she typed in her daughter's name, James. She loved that the list seemed to describe James' personality despite the fact that it is traditionally a boy's name. She printed the list on pink cardstock and included the story behind the list in a pocket made from patterned paper.

Alison Chabe, Charlestown, Massachusetts

Supplies: Patterned papers, tag and flower tack (Chatterbox); letter stamps (Delta, Hero Arts); mesh (Magic Mesh); pink, rose and orange cardstocks; black and pink stamping inks; extra thick embossing powder; ribbon; library card; library card pocket

Holly

Teri-Lyn caught the essence of her middle daughter on this beach-themed design. She soaked cheesecloth in walnut ink to stain it, adding greater dimension and visual interest to this beachcombers' delight.

Teri-Lyn Masters, Truro, Nova Scotia, Canada

Supplies: Patterned papers (Leaving Prints); letter stamps, stipple shell stamps and shells wheel, caramel-colored ink and eyelets (Stampin' Up!); brown, olive and cream cardstocks; cheesecloth; twine beach netting

O is for Ocean

ocean (o´ shen) n. the great body of salt water that covers approximately 71% of the surface of the earth

The Girls of Summer

To keep her title from appearing washed out on this layout, Gayla stamped title letters with white acrylic paint, then stamped again with brown stamping ink. She then brushed walnut ink on the letters to add a sun-kissed glow.

Gayla Feachen, Grapevine, Texas

Supplies: Patterned papers (K & Company); laminate chip tag (Club Scrap); beach-themed and definition stickers (K & Company, Making Memories); metal label holder (Li'l Davis Designs); rivets (Chatterbox); letter and date stamps, brads (Making Memories); metal rimmed circle tags (Office Max); jute fabric; fibers; vintage photo and walnut stain

A Perfect Moment

Cari kept her layout simple to keep the focus on how the power of the ocean can stop even the most energetic in their tracks. The floral patterned paper captures the motion of the waves, while the cream print plays up the tones and textures of the beach. Several well-placed metal accents unify the black-and-white photo with the page.

Cari Locken, Edmonton, Alberta, Canada

Supplies: Patterned papers (Anna Griffin, 7 Gypsies); ribbon (Offray); letter sticker (Creative Imaginations); flower brads, dragonfly plaque, metal letter charms and black cardstock (Making Memories)

Oceanside

Preprinted transparencies featuring seashells were the perfect embellishment for Pamela's oceanside page. She placed beach-themed word stickers in the center of the page, allowing them to overlap the images above and below.

Pamela James, Ventura, California

Supplies: Patterned transparencies and word stickers (Creative Imaginations); blue and white cardstocks; fibers; charms; shells; black pen

Matthew's First Trip to the Ocean

The subdued colors of the ocean are captured on Cindy's page, highlighting her son's first trip to the ocean. A metal-rimmed tag, jute and die cut add hints of treasure to this peaceful design.

Cindy Rollins, Cleveland, Texas

Supplies: Patterned papers (Chatterbox); metal-rimmed tag, vellum, jute and antique mini brads (Making Memories); tag and starfish die cuts (Sizzix); letter stamp sticker (Creative Imaginations) brown cardstock

Danielle

The hidden treasure of bonus photos waits inside the creative captain's-log-style mini album on Tammy's page. For the binding, she pierced the spine with paper precor and threaded fibers through the holes. Torn strips of paper create a frame for the focal-point photo.

Tammy Gauck, Jenison, Michigan

Supplies: Patterned papers (Making Memories); compass stamp (Inkadinkado); clock stamp (Stampabilities); fibers (Fibers By The Yard); buttons (Jesse James); letters (Foofala); tag; postage stamp; brown stamping ink; aqua cardstock

As You Journey Through Life...

Martha designed this layout to encourage her son to wander the least-traveled paths of life, as her map patterned paper background illustrates. A small silk bag of shells accents the photo.

Martha Crowther, Salem, New Hampshire

Supplies: Patterned paper (Cut-It-Up); silk bag (Michaels); green and cream cardstocks; transparency; corrugated cardboard; shells; bottle charms; wire; fibers; vellum

Magic Beside the Sea

Burlap stretches across this page like the expanse of the sandy beach along the water's edge. A printed transparency gives the illusion that text is printed directly on a photo.

Rhonda Bonifay, Virginia Beach, Virginia

Supplies: Metal label holder, definition and ribbon (Making Memories); photo mat (Wal-Mart); twine; burlap; transparency; light blue cardstock

First Beach Experience

Melodee showcased her beach baby's first experience at the shore by sanding and painting the title, photo and layout edges to mimic the crashing waves. She applied extra thick embossing powder to beach elements in a small shadow box to give them a "washed up" look.

Melodee Langworthy, Rockford, Michigan

Supplies: Patterned paper (Sweetwater); definition words and washer (Making Memories); small metal frame, metal clips and glass bottle (7 Gypsies); stamps (Ma Vinci's Reliquary, Stampin' Up!); chalk; brown stamping ink; transparency; acrylic paint; jute; seashells; sand; drywall tape; eyelets; envelope

Siblings

After numerous attempts of trying to get her children to hold hands on the beach for a picture, Lisa gave up, only to find them clasping hands on their own just a few days later! She designed this digital layout to celebrate the special sibling bond that her children, only one year apart, share.

Lisa Winzeler, West Unity, Ohio

Supplies: Image-editing software (Adobe Photoshop)

Sand Dollar

When Michele received a sand dollar charm from a friend, she knew a scrapbook page was in the works! She chose a purple background to coordinate with the live, fuzzy purple sand dollars in the photo, and then embossed the background with silver powder for a splash of excitement.

Michele Reed, Vista, California

Supplies: Patterned papers (Design Originals); stamps (Stampin' Up!); lettering template (QuicKutz); fibers (Fibers By The Yard); safety pin (Making Memories); silver envelope (EK Success); silver pen; embossing ink; purple, cream and light blue cardstocks; silver embossing powder; sand dollar charm

South Padre Island

Kari designed everything on this layout digitally, even the ribbon, tag and vellum. She based her design on a sketch from a scrapbooking Web site.

Kari Schoonover, Schertz, Texas
Photos: Chris Sherman, Sylvania, Ohio

Supplies: Image-editing software (Microsoft Digital Image Pro); label maker images (www.acme.com); brad image (www.Scrapbook-Bytes.com)

Time Stands Still

Margert folded up her thoughts on this day at the beach neatly inside a small red file folder. The compass nailhead and bold, red letters add dynamic strength to the layout.

Margert Ann Kruljac, Newnan, Georgia

Supplies: Patterned papers (Colors by Design, Daisy D's, Rusty Pickle); foam stamps, rub-ons and acrylic paint (Making Memories); compass nailhead (Magic Scraps); twill tape (source unknown); red and white cardstocks; red stamping ink; transparency; black pen

Glorious Green Goggles

White and green cardstocks were all that Bonnie needed for a layout that showcases her son's vacation staple—green goggles. Using extra photos of Max taken from a distance, Bonnie assembled small photo mosaics in two corners.

Bonnie Gokey, Sugar Hill, Georgia

Supplies: Square punch (Creative Memories); green, light green and white cardstocks

Summer

Lynn's response to using black-and-white film in her new camera was this cheerful layout, created by layering a few strips of bright papers. She used up extra ribbon pieces to dress up the page and draw attention to the title.

Lynn Whelan, Savannah, Georgia

Supplies: Patterned papers (Carolee's Creations); ribbons (Offray); letter die cuts (source unknown)

The Wave

Tisha highlighted a day at the beach by framing photos with patterned paper, then tearing and rolling back the edges. She applied glaze to flower punches for added shine.

Tisha McCuiston, Mechanicsville, Virginia

Supplies: Patterned papers (Chatterbox); square and tag die cuts (QuicKutz); letter buttons (Junkitz); flower sticker (source unknown); stenciled definition stamp (source unknown); rub-on letters (Making Memories); brads; daisy and vine punches; fibers; straight pins; clear glaze; drywall tape

P is for Prayer

prayer (prer) n. that act or practice of praying, as to a god

Happiness

To illustrate her chaotic life, Maegan cut her photo into pieces, glued them to wooden squares, inked the edges and arranged them like a puzzle. She chose a rich, yellow color scheme and a comforting Bible verse to represent the restoration of happiness in her life.

Maegan Hall, Virginia Beach, Virginia
Photo: Amy Bare, Chesapeake, Virginia

Supplies: Patterned papers (Karen Foster Design, Paper Adventures, Penny Black); decorative paper (Paper Adventures); stickers (Karen Foster Design); wooden squares (Scrapfindings); flower accents (www.memoriesoftherabbit.com); fibers (Fibers By The Yard); rub-ons, tag and buttons (Making Memories); yellow cardstocks (Making Memories, Paper Garden); punches (EK Success, Punch Bunch)

Deliverance

Linda bound up a black-and-white photo with ribbon, thread and lots of love. She pieced together warm, visually textured patterns and incorporated stitching for a timeless, quiltlike effect.

Linda Albrecht, St. Peter, Minnesota

Supplies: Patterned papers (Provo Craft); journaling tag paper (SEI); ribbon (Michaels); brads (Making Memories); button and thread (Hobby Lobby); rickrack (Jo-Ann Fabrics); photo corner (Magenta); heart charm (source unknown); jewelry tag; walnut ink; sewing machine

Amen

Tarri captured her son during his bedtime prayers to document an important part of his life. She used a label maker to make a favorite Bible verse stand out on a green background.

Tarri Botwinski, Grand Rapids, Michigan

Supplies: Patterned papers (Treehouse Designs, 7 Gypsies); eyelets (Making Memories); letter stamps (PSX Design); label maker (Dymo); black and white cardstocks; black stamping ink

The Path of Life

Stacie felt this photo of her youngest son, new to the journey of life, would be perfect to highlight this powerful piece of Scripture. She added her own journaling to laminate chips from the hardware store and threaded ribbon through the tops of each.

Stacie Gammill, Sulphur Springs, Texas

Supplies: Patterned papers (K & Company, Karen Foster Design, Paper Adventures, Pebbles, 7 Gypsies); typewriter key letter stickers and word stickers (K & Company); ribbon (Making Memories); photo corners and small gold frame (Nunn Design); laminate chips (Home Depot)

A Child's Beauty

Deanna incorporated the colors of a sunset into the design of this page. Letter tiles coordinate perfectly with patterned paper and journaling shows reverence.

Deanna Koontz, Petersburg, Indiana
Photo: Darrel Koontz, Petersburg, Indiana

Supplies: Patterned paper and title letter tiles (Doodlebug Design); title rub-ons (Making Memories); fibers (Fibers By The Yard); black and peach cardstocks; chalk

Family Scripture Study

From the patterned paper to the printed twill, the power of words ignites this page dedicated to Sam's family Scripture study. To print on twill tape, Sam printed words on paper first, then adhered the twill tape over the words and ran it through the printer again for perfect placement.

Sam Cousins, Trumbull, Connecticut

Supplies: Patterned paper (Karen Foster Design); letter stickers (Creative Imaginations); definition stickers and black mini brads (Making Memories); black stamping ink; black cardstock; transparency

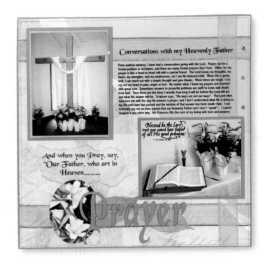

Prayer

Pamela designed a formal-looking page using pastel blues and gold accents to pour out her reverence toward prayer. She printed her journaling on a transparency and lined up the heading with a strip of ribbon to make it appear as if the words were printed on the ribbon.

Pamela James, Ventura, California

Supplies: Patterned papers (Autumn Leaves, NRN Designs); gold paper (Paper Adventures); skeleton leaves (Target); gold brads; light blue and periwinkle cardstocks; ribbons; blue stamping ink; vellum; transparency; sewing machine

Have Faith

Tricia's collage-style design is powered by the simple faith of a child. Button accents keep a childlike spirit shining through, while more elaborate charms, crackle and distressing techniques evoke a sense of spiritual maturity.

Tricia Rubens, Castle Rock, Colorado

Supplies: Patterned papers (K & Company, Rusty Pickle); letter and frame stickers (Creative Imaginations); ribbon and tin photo corners (Making Memories); clock hand (EK Success); dove charm (Westrim); pewter heart charm (Magenta); faith charm (Darice); fleur-de-lis charm (Memory Lane); tag (Me & My Big Ideas); crackle medium (Plaid); pressed tin (Artistic Expressions); black stamping ink; acrylic paint; buttons; vellum

Create in Me A Pure Heart...

A single patterned paper sheet that looks like many patterns were pieced together forms the background of Robin's layout. She framed a photo of her son by applying a black ink pad around the edges, then added gold ink over the black once it was partially dry.

Robin Hohenstern, Brooklyn Park, Minnesota

Supplies: Patterned papers (Li'l Davis Designs); script rubber stamp (Inkadinkado); gold corner accent (ARTchix Studio); letter stickers (Pebbles); ribbon; library pocket; black and gold stamping inks; date stamp; gray and brown stamping inks; tag; tan cardstock; sewing machine

1 Peter 3:3-4

A mother's prayer for her daughter is captured here on layered tags, listing the Scripture reference on top, a note to her daughter in the middle and finally the printed verse as the buried treasure. Maegan used ornate charms to accentuate the verse's focus.

Maegan Hall, Virginia Beach, Virginia

Supplies: Patterned papers (Autumn Leaves, Pebbles, 7 Gypsies); rubber stamps (PSX Design); library card envelope (www.memoriesoftherabbit.com); round metal charm and photo corner (www.maudeandmillie.com); tags (Rusty Pickle, 7 Gypsies); aged ribbon and belt clip (Scrapfindings); brown cardstock; brown stamping ink

"Ask
and it will be
given to you;
seek
and you will
find;
knock
and the door
will be
opened to
you. For
everyone who
asks
receives; he
who
seeks
finds; and to
him who
knocks,
the door will
be opened."

MATTHEW 7:7-8

October 2003

Ask...

The faith of children radiate off this peacefully pleasing page. Melissa embellished only with a shimmering ribbon and charm to firmly ground the simple design.

Melissa Diekema, Grand Rapids, Michigan

Supplies: Patterned Paper (K & Company); ribbon (Stampin' Up!); rectangle nickel charm (7 Gypsies); brown stamping ink; sage and cream speckled cardstocks; date stamp; transparency

The Greatest Gift

Michelle created a digital design to showcase a layout her husband made for her, complete with a poem he wrote. She added paper, embellishment and template images from CDs on her page.

Michelle Shefveland, Sauk Rapids, Minnesota

Supplies: Image-editing software (Adobe Photoshop Elements); background paper and heart charm images (Simply Stated CD, www.CottageArts.net); torn music paper and fibers images (Simply Shabby CD, www.CottageArts.net)

Dear God...

Amy expressed prayerful gratitude for her family on this soft and sweet layout. She printed her photo in tones that match the patterned papers and created her own patterned paper by stamping with watermark ink and foam letter stamps.

Amy Howe, Frisco, Texas

Supplies: Patterned papers, border strips, green tacks, tag and love tiles (Chatterbox); rubber stamps (PSX Design); stamping ink; foam stamps (Making Memories); sage, olive, purple and yellow cardstocks; black pen; black stamping and watermark inks; sewing machine

P is for Play

play (plá) n. to amuse oneself, as by taking part in a game or sport; engage in recreation

Around the Park

Heather's circular page design plays up the idea of her title. She punched circles from white cardstock to frame three smaller photos of her son and hand stitched around the design element with contrasting thread colors.

Heather Coleman, Williamsburg, Virginia

Supplies: Patterned papers (Bo-Bunny Press, Chatterbox, SEI); suede decorative paper (Wintech); black, sage and white cardstocks; black and white threads; date stamp; vellum

Prospect Park

Melissa added whimsical dimension to the background of this page with shadow ink, letter stamps and stickers. She layered patterned paper, a script transparency and a piece of patterned vellum to achieve the pattern on the right side of the page.

Melissa C. Thigpen, Columbia, South Carolina

Supplies: Patterned papers, striped vellum, letter stickers, and blue and tan nails (Chatterbox); letter stamps (Ma Vinci's Reliquary); green shadow ink (Hero Arts); script transparency (7 Gypsies); transparency (3M); tan cardstock; foam tape

Celebration

Dee's scrapbook page takes a visual recess to release vibrant energy through loud, playful colors and patterns. Journaling about celebrating who you are hides behind the lower right-hand photo.

Dee Gallimore-Perry, Griswold, Connecticut

Supplies: Patterned papers, circle tag die cut, small frame and block (KI Memories); metal ball chain, title rub-ons and definition (Making Memories); epoxy letters (K & Company); letter stamps (PSX Design); letter sticker (Creative Imaginations); black stamping ink; chalk; sewing machine

Art in Motion

Kelly repeated the playful photo of her son in a pop-art fashion. She created a lengthy label maker strip in "ticker style" and placed it across the top of the page.

Kelly Goree, Shelbyville, Kentucky

Supplies: Patterned paper and mini frames (KI Memories); white letter stickers (Chatterbox); title letter template (EK Success); label maker label (Dymo); black and white cardstocks

Jump, Jump, Skip, Smile

The joy of spring break comes alive on this page through brilliant red cardstock and a photo taken from a unique vantage point. A decorated library pocket houses Lisa's journaling.

Lisa Mote, Murfreesboro, Tennessee

Supplies: Patterned paper (Li'l Davis Designs); torn paper edge and dot stamps (Stampotique Originals); ; red stamping ink; "buds" metal word (Making Memories); letter stencil (Autumn Leaves); label maker (Dymo); cardstock; dyes; vintage measuring tape; black stamping ink

Kids at Play

Wanting to reflect the same fun and youthful vibrancy of the day spent with friends at the park, Stacie layered colorful circles and strips of paper over an energetic backdrop. Words positioned at different angles lend a childlike quality to the title.

Stacie Gammill, Sulphur Springs, Texas

Supplies: Patterned papers (Paper Loft, Sweetwater); textured papers, copper letter brads and pewter letter charm (Provo Craft); license plate letter stickers (Sticker Studio); foam letter stamps (Target); antique lowercase letter stamps (PSX Design); label maker (Dymo); black acrylic paint; photo turn

On the Move

Sepia-toned photos capture the essence of a boy at play. Postage stamp and travel-themed stickers help capture the idea of being "on the move."

Martha Crowther, Salem, New Hampshire

Supplies: Patterned papers, postcard and stickers (Patchwork Paper); fiber (Fibers By The Yard); ribbon; twill (source unknown); family and friends circle (source unknown); black and white cardstocks; transparency

Slide

An art inspiration challenge Tracy participated in on a Web site produced this energetic layout. She sanded her letter stickers for interest.

Tracy Clements, Smithville, Ontario, Canada

Supplies: Letter stickers (Creative Imaginations); colored brads (Making Memories); purple, yellow, burnt orange, lavender and lime cardstocks; sandpaper

Sandbox

Inspired by the happy colors in her photos, Megan played up the childhood charm in this layout with nostalgic ephemera and primary colors. Stamped twill tape adds a playful title across the top.

Megan Friesen, Chilliwack, British Columbia, Canada

Supplies: Patterned paper (K & Company); patterned tissue paper and ticket (DMD); metal washers (Jest Charming); antique letter stamps (PSX Design); label stickers (Pebbles); clear definition sticker (Making Memories); spirit charm (Scrapheap Re³); bottle cap (Li'l Davis Designs); brown stamping ink; twill tape; brads

The Swing

Julie put the readers of her album into the flyer's seat by creating a swinging title from a piece of chain and multiple tags. Her focal-point photo makes it seem as if you are swinging right along with the subject.

Julie Marie Hickey, Keswick, Ontario, Canada

Supplies: Patterned papers (Daisy D's); letter stamps (Making Memories, PSX Design); green ribbon (Making Memories); tags (www.twopeasinabucket.com); chain (hardware store); white cardstock (SEI); black, blue, green and brown stamping inks; silver embossing powder

Of All the Animals...

Nicola allowed the playful shapes and colors of her photos to bounce and giggle across this page through the repetition of circles and lines. Various brads and eyelets are scattered throughout the design.

Nicola Clarke, Basildon, Essex, England

Supplies: Brads and eyelets (Making Memories); acrylic words (Junkitz); paper embellishment (KI Memories); quote (Autumn Leaves, Quote/Unquote); thread; circle punches; sewing machine; textured brown, orange, light orange and green cardstocks

Jungle Gym

Playing off of the design of the jungle gym in the photo, Nancy cut strips and shapes that allow the equipment to climb across the entire page. Smaller circles were placed between her title letters to coordinate.

Nancy Rogers, Baton Rouge, Louisiana

Supplies: Patterned paper (Paper Fever); lettering template (Scrap Pagerz); red, gray and black cardstocks; chalk

Playing Is Hard Work

Shannon loved this exhausted-looking image of her son after he had played for 20 minutes on playground equipment, and couldn't help focusing on what "hard work" it is to play. She silhouetted the main photo and created burlap texture with image-editing software.

Shannon Freeman, Bellingham, Washington

Supplies: Drawing program (MicroGrafx Draw); image-editing software (Microsoft Photo Editor, Microsoft Paint)

Q is for Quiet

quiet (kwi´ et) adj. still; calm; motionless

A Moment in Time

Amy took this photo of her daughter at the exact moment she turned 3. She sanded all patterned papers for a more subdued quality. Her title was handcut, then embossed with gold powder.

Amy Stultz, Mooresville, Indiana

Supplies: Patterned paper (K & Company); decorative textured paper (Jennifer Collection); metal label holder (www.maude andmillie.com); ribbon (Offray); brown stamping ink; gold embossing powder

Joyful…

Suzy cut a patterned paper sheet into separate blocks in order to leave quiet space in between the designs. In the open spaces, she place rub-on words that describe her daughter.

Suzy West, Fremont, California

Supplies: Patterned paper (K & Company); rub-on words (Making Memories); silk flower; corrugated cardboard; green cardstock

Always Believe

A tranquil green backdrop draws out the sense of reflection from this black-and-white photo framed with stark white matting. Michele wound dark green thread around a lighter green strip for a subtle hint of texture.

Michele Woods, Reynoldsburg, Ohio

Supplies: Patterned paper (Creative Imaginations); woven label (Me & My Big Ideas); fibers; green and white cardstocks

Dare to Dream

A unique photographic angle lends a pensive quality to this page. By layering cardstocks and patterned papers at different angles, a mere label and a shimmering ribbon are all the embellishment needed for this page's sweet success.

Ricki Chambers, Hurricane, Utah

Supplies: Patterned paper and decorative paper (Rusty Pickle); ribbon (Wal-Mart); rub-ons (Making Memories); label maker labels (Dymo); pink and neutral cardstocks; black stamping ink

Reflections

Peggy was inspired to create this layout after printing out photos of her son and realizing how quickly he is growing up. Wave patterned paper and pewter letters perfectly capture the memory of throwing rocks in the lake that day.

Peggy Sue Slocum, Duluth, Minnesota

Supplies: Patterned paper (Wübie); metal frames, eyelet phrases and eyelet letters (Making Memories); vellum (NRN Designs); black cardstock; eyelets

What Lies Before Us...

Soft-spoken beauty is accentuated in muted tones on Amy's layout of her daughter's reflective moment. A quote sticker, which Amy layered over torn patterned paper, fit perfectly with the mood she wanted to create.

Amy Howe, Frisco, Texas

Supplies: Patterned papers and rub-on letter (Creative Imaginations); snaptape (www.ScrapAddict.com); quote sticker (Wordsworth); metal mesh and snap (Making Memories); black pen; gray paper; white cardstock

Moments of Solitude

Alison cut cardstock strips for her background and inked the edges to give each stripe a space of its own. Rub-on words and a clear page pebble finish the simple design.

Alison Marquis, Pleasant Grove, Utah

Supplies: Rub-on words (Making Memories); page pebble (K & Company); black, white, blue, light blue, green, orange and yellow cardstocks; black stamping ink

Talking to Geese

Becky documented her daughter Kristin's youthful optimism by journaling about the time Kristin believed she could communicate with geese. Combining black-and-white photos with color photos captures the mood of an autumn day and works well with the peaceful open space of the spread.

Becky Thompson, Fruitland, Idaho

Supplies: Patterned paper (Rusty Pickle); preprinted transparency (Creative Imaginations); die-cut letters (QuicKutz); natural, pink and navy blue cardstocks

Youth

Sande's backdrop of gold embossed patterned papers adds brilliance to this time-pausing page. Inspiring words inside slide mounts covered in patterned paper balance the weight created by the striking photograph.

Sande Krieger, Salt Lake City, Utah

Supplies: Embossed patterned paper (Artistic Scrapper); patterned paper (Chatterbox); slide mounts (Magic Scraps); tags, clock faces and ribbon (Making Memories); cross stitch fabric (Jo-Ann Fabrics); ribbon (May Arts); metal label holder (Nunn Design); heart and jump ring; dimensional adhesive

I want to sit around your *LIFE*

and breathe your *AIR*

I Want to Sit...

Barbara used a song lyric as the inspiration for her title and designed her page around it. Premade letter tiles, corner accents and a butterfly embellishment bring out the light tones in the patterned paper and photograph.

Barbara Pfeffer, Omaha, Nebraska

Supplies: Patterned paper (7 Gypsies); tiles, photo corners, heart accent and rub-on letters (EK Success); black stamping ink

It's just a line from an obscure love song ("Hey Girl" by O.A.R.) but it so perfectly describes what it's like to be your mother at this stage in your life. We're so frequently on the go, but when we're not, in those quiet moments at home, it's a true blessing to watch you as you go about your life. You are such a sweet, joyful little boy. Sometimes all I do, sometimes all I **can** do, is to sit there, as the beds go unmade and the dishes pile up, watching you play, discover, grow. I sit there, ready for you to climb in my lap to read a few pages of a book or to propel yourself into my arms for a quick hug, before you toddle off again. Just sitting around your life and breathing your air. And I am happy.

It's in the Eyes

Demure colors reflecting a lighthearted innocence are layered and inked for a sense of intrigue as deep as this child's eyes. Amy stamped corner designs with paint, allowing them to overlap her photo, metal mesh and ribbon.

Amy Goldstein, Kent Lakes, New York

Supplies: Patterned paper (Scenic Route Paper Co.); metal mesh, photo corners, blossoms and stamps (Making Memories); modeling paste (Golden); letter stickers (Creative Imaginations); round title charms (Manto Fev); ribbon (Offray); cardstock; paint

r R is for Rain

rain (rane) n. water falling to earth in droplets larger than 0.5mm

Stormy Weather

A blustery barrage of patterned vellum over speckled cardstock, in conjunction with decorated die cuts, sets the stage for Michelle's photos of a day caught out in the storm. Tree die cuts exceed the edges of a tag for a wind-blown effect.

Michelle Hubbartt, Grand Junction, Colorado

Supplies: Patterned vellum and papers (Club Scrap); blue mesh (Magenta); large tag and metal-rimmed tags (Making Memories); cloud and small tree punches (Emagination Crafts); dragonfly punch (McGill); tree die cuts (EK Success); speckled cardstock; gold brad; extra thick embossing powder; chalk; blue and brown stamping inks

Rainy Day

Who wants the rain to go away when you can have as much fun as Michelle's kids? Michelle drew out the children's umbrella and raincoat colors for her page design and accented the spread with playful yellow buttons.

Michelle Maret, South Bend, Indiana

Supplies: Patterned paper (Provo Craft); yellow burlap (Once Upon a Scribble); die-cut letters and tag (QuicKutz); buttons (EK Success); brown stamping ink; black and red cardstocks; mesh (handmade); fibers; thread

Raindrops on My Fingertips

One small photo speaks volumes on this impactful page. Desiree designed the layout so that she and her son could look back to see that even the simplest things can be pleasurable and fun.

Desiree McClellan, Decatur, Alabama

Supplies: Textured olive, light green, black and cream cardstocks; date stamp (Office Max)

Kayla in the Rain

Ribbons and frills abound on Angelia's page dedicated to capturing the girly feeling of fun. She cut a photo of her daughter's boots into a tag shape and layered it over a larger journaling tag.

Angelia Wigginton, Belmont, Mississippi

Supplies: Patterned paper (Li'l Davis Designs); black snaps and metal letter charms (Making Memories); colored jump rings (Junkitz); round letter stickers (Chatterbox); title letter stickers (Doodlebug Design); letter stamps (Rubber Stampede); black stamping ink; rickrack; ribbon; silk flower; pink cardstock

Diggin' Dirt

Tisha made a mud-lovin' masterpiece by distressing dirt-bike patterned paper and adding her own smudges, scratches and all-boy effects. Splashes of gold ink across tan cardstock help these messy moments of childhood shine as the treasures they are.

Tisha McCuiston, Mechanicsville, Virginia

Supplies: Patterned paper and statement stickers (Karen Foster Design); peach cardstock; gold stamping ink

Rain

Her daughter's concern for the birds caught out in the rain in-spired Teresa's design. White eyelash fibers give a feather-light effect and add visually stimulating texture to the page.

Teresa L. Olier, Colorado Springs, Colorado

Supplies: Textured silver paper (Emagination Crafts); white eyelash fiber (Fibers By The Yard); mini square letters (Making Memories); black and light blue cardstocks; vellum

R is for Remember and Reminisce

re•mem•ber (ri mem´ ber) v. to have (an event, thing, person, etc.) come to mind again
rem•i•nisce (rem´e nis´) v. to think, talk, or write about remembered events or experiences

Remembering the Wigleys

Nostalgic patterns sewn into place against warm colors add homespun appeal to Amy's heritage layout. She dangled tags from fibers to label each person in the photo. An assortment of letter stickers on a strip of burlap form the title.

Amy Brown, Eclectic, Alabama

Supplies: Patterned papers (Provo Craft, Rusty Pickle); double tag shapes (QuicKutz); letter stickers (Creative Imaginations); fibers (Scrapping With Style); nailheads (Jest Charming); gold clip; rust, olive and cream speckled cardstocks; burlap; wire mesh; green stamping ink

Ranta Family History

Darlene designed this spread using all the family history her grandmother had recorded. She imprinted her great-grandmother's maiden and married names on each page by heating a leatherlike foam sheet and stamping letters into the material.

Darlene Johnson Calloway, Tequesta, Florida

Supplies: Leatherlike foam sheet (Commotion); patterned paper (source unknown); letter stamps (Club Scrap); tan handmade paper; frame die cuts (Sizzix); postcards (Creative Imaginations); brown cardstock; brown water color paint; mustard, sepia, olive and espresso inks; brown foam; chalks

Rustic

While observing the ruins of a dilapidated building on the Delta, Shelby was reminded that there is always more than meets the eye, as a mother duck and her brood came strutting from inside. She designed this page as a reminder to look for the extraordinary in the ordinary all around her.

Shelby Valadez, Saugus, California

Supplies: Watercolor paper (Canson); patterned papers (Chatterbox, 7 Gypsies); patterned transparency and metal label holder (Magic Scraps); foam stamp (Jo-Ann Fabrics); transparency; black stamping ink

The Way Things Were

This photograph of Holly's grandfather called for a simple page to preserve her child-hood memories of him in the cotton fields. She enlarged a photo twice on patterned paper, then trimmed one copy and placed the two next to each other for a continuous background. She then mounted the smaller photo on black foam.

Holly Pittroff, Huntersville, North Carolina

Supplies: Patterned paper (Karen Foster Design); flexi-foam (Fibre Craft); metal-rimmed tag and eyelet (Making Memories); cardstock; fiber; vellum; brown stamping inks

Alice in Her Garden

Carolyn arranged a bouquet of memories on this floral-themed page showcasing her grandmother's green thumb. She printed her journaling onto three cards and attached them to tags. Two of the journaling cards rotate around the brad in order to more easily read both sections.

Carolyn Cleveland, Maysville, Georgia

Supplies: Patterned paper; tan, rust, taupe and cream cardstocks; die cuts; letter stickers, stencil, tag and twill (Club Scrap); garden stickers (Colorbök); flower stickers (Creative Imaginations); letter "A" sticker and typewriter letter stickers (EK Success); word sticker (Chatterbox); square brads (Making Memories); fibers (www.Annalisse.com); library pocket (source unknown); black stamping ink

Mama and Grandpa Early 1940s

Kathie remembers her mother with a sentimental collage of different elements. She used fringe, buttons, ribbon and metal accents on a tag for a comfortable, homespun feel.

Kathie Fracaro, Hixson, Tennessee

Supplies: Patterned papers (K & Company, Keeping Memories Alive, 7 Gypsies); small envelope (DMD); metal word and wire heart (Making Memories); letter stamps (Hero Arts); flower heart charm (source unknown); pink trim; buttons; tag; chalk; gold clips; ribbon; brown stamping ink

Anthony Lehman, U.S. Navy

World War II memories stand at attention in Barb's tribute to her grandfather. Her journaling is hidden beneath a hinged element with a quote sticker on top, giving the entire spread the feel of a traveling trunk with a story to tell.

Barb Hogan, Cincinnati, Ohio

Supplies: Patterned papers (Rusty Pickle); postage and letter stickers (EK Success); quote sticker (Wordsworth); hinges (Making Memories); tan, gray and cream cardstocks; brown stamping ink; pen

My grandfather, Tony Lehman, served his country during WWII in the US Navy in the Admiralty Islands. Unfortunately, life on these islands in the south Pacific, just north of New Guinea, wasn't exactly as romantic as it was portrayed in the musical "South Pacific". The days were long and hot, the work was hard, the bugs

were bad, and there was no Bali Hai. However, like Nellie, the "cockeyed optimist" heroine in the movie, my grandpa never lost his sense of humor. He was well known for sketching scenes or writing jokes on coconuts and mailing them back to the family in Ohio. Many of these silly "war coconuts" are still in the family.

Grandpa and Grandma

Janice used her grandparents' wedding photo, matted 6 times, as a launching point for this heartfelt collage. She collaged four different patterns of paper together, placing a large cut-out heart on top and then using black mesh and lace for her borders.

Janice Dodson, Cookeville, Tennessee

Supplies: Patterned papers (Daisy D's, Li'l Davis Designs); pocket and tag (Daisy D's); letter stickers (Making Memories, Paper Adventures); black mesh, fibers, golden gem brad (Magic Scraps); tan pocket mesh (Magic Mesh); black lace and twine (Wal-Mart); keys (EK Success); tea dye stamping ink (Ranger); black and cream cardstocks; safety pin; foam tape

Behind the Name

The rich history behind Peggy's family name in Ireland is formatted into this scrapbook page with storybook flair. She found an image of her surname's coat of arms online, copied and pasted it into Microsoft Word, printed it on cardstock and accented it with walnut and brown inks.

Peggy Roarty, Council Bluffs, Iowa

Supplies: Patterned papers (Karen Foster Design); backgammon board stamp (River City Rubber Works); watch face (Maya Road); watch hands and cover (Manto Fev); metal door knocker charms (source unknown); metal heart charm (source unknown); black tape; red and black cardstocks; brads; brown stamping ink; walnut ink

Gone But Never Forgotten

Melonie designed this layout as a memorial to her great uncle—a gift for her grandpa in remembrance of his brother. Numerous patterned papers, patriotic accents, brads and raffia come together for a heritage look.

Melonie Robinson, Merrill, Wisconsin

Supplies: Patterned papers (K & Company, Paper Patch); rub-on title letters (Making Memories); badge (Li'l Davis Designs); letter stickers (Mrs. Grossman's); tag; red cardstock; eyelet; brads; black stamping ink; raffia; foam tape

Joe Underriter

Julie designed this layout in memory of her dad. She scanned and printed the cover of his military class book onto a transparency and laid it over his graduation photo.

Julie K. Eickmeier, Fort Myers, Florida

Supplies: Letter stickers (Mrs. Grossman's); stencils (U.S. Stamp & Sign); army green cardstock; transparency

Chevy

Family vehicles are often as beloved as family members, as is demonstrated here on Dottie's page. Her layout combines new and vintage elements, just like a photo of an old truck taken in the present day.

Dottie Clark, Belleair, Florida

Supplies: Patterned paper and photo turn (7 Gypsies); letter stencil (Autumn Leaves); wooden letters (Li'l Davis Designs); ribbon (Making Memories); label maker labels (Dymo); subway token, key, game piece numbers and optometrist glass lens (found items); black, red and black cardstocks; foam tape

S is for Sleeping

sleep•ing (slep´ ing) n. a natural, regularly recurring condition of rest for the body and mind

Suspend Time

Inspired by an art piece with the same title, Bela designed this page of her babe in slumberland using colors from her inspiration source. She triple embossed the block of terra cotta paper beneath the title with clear extra thick embossing powder for a glossy finish.

Bela Luis, Winnipeg, Manitoba, Canada
Photo: Joel Ross Photography, Winnipeg, Manitoba, Canada

Supplies: Patterned papers (K & Company); tag (Foofala); skeleton leaves (All Night Media); paper clip and metal clock (7 Gypsies); clock stamp (Inkadinkado); black, white and cream cardstocks; brad; black stamping ink; extra thick embossing powder

Patience

Wendy captured the essence of a lunchtime snooze on this page. She added a childlike quality by stamping the letter "E" backward on twill, and scattered blocks cut from a patterned paper across the page.

Wendy Bickford, Antelope, California

Supplies: Patterned papers (Karen Foster Design, Pebbles, Rusty Pickle); twill tape (Creek Bank Creations); letter stamps (K & Company); buttons (Junkitz); satin ribbon; red and black cardstocks; black stamping ink

Remember This

Exhausted from the excitement of vacation, Jlyne's two sons sleep blissfully on this bold-colored page. Black-and-white patterned papers and accents awaken the photo and coordinate with the inked boundaries of the background.

Jlyne Hanback, Biloxi, Mississippi

Supplies: Patterned papers (DMD, Frances Meyer, KI Memories, 7 Gypsies); rub-on words and metal-rimmed vellum circle tag (Making Memories); clock charm (Manto Fev); die-cut rectangle (KI Memories); letter stamps (Hero Arts); black stamping ink

Girl With a Curl

Melanie gave this layout the look of covers pulled snuggly around a pillow-framed image, perfect for a photo of her sleeping daughter. She printed a nursery rhyme on transparency and added cardstock nursery rhyme stickers to give the page bedtime-story style.

Melanie Howard, Kanehsatake, Quebec, Canada

Supplies: Patterned paper (Daisy D's); nursery rhyme cardstock and letter stickers, large and small mailing tags (Rusty Pickle); spiral clip, eyelet number charm, mini brads (Making Memories); dragonfly brad (www.theembellishmentstore.com); pink gingham ribbon (Offray); ribbons; twine; black pen; black stamping ink

So Sweet

When Shari's daughter chose an unusual place to take a nap, she wanted to create a simple layout to keep the focus on the humorous and sweet photo. A single band of striped paper at the bottom grounds Shari's layout, and letter stickers make up the title.

Shari Barnes, Burlington, Kentucky

Supplies: Patterned paper (Chatterbox); letter stickers (KI Memories); letter stamps (Hero Arts); white stamping ink; brown cardstock

Aaron & Lucy Catnappin'

Sheila digitally composed this layout using hues and patterns from the couch and shirt in the photograph. She used filters to create a golden sheen and add furry texture to the words.

Sheila Mcintosh Dixon, Milton, Florida

Supplies: Image-editing software (Adobe Photoshop Elements, Jasc Paint Shop Pro, Microsoft Digital Image Pro)

Twist 2 Sleep

Stacy's daughter twists her hair as she falls asleep, which became the focus of this page. For the black file-folder page element, Stacy sanded a card template, applied watermark ink, immediately sprinkling with black embossing powder and repeated several times.

Stacy Yoder, Yucaipa, California

Supplies: Pink embossed paper (Paper Adventures); card template (Deluxe Designs); black mesh paper (Magenta); textured papers (Jennifer Collection, Provo Craft, Starr Papers); title, number and name stickers (Sticker Studio); metal mesh, rub-ons, washer words and safety pins (Making Memories); flower sticker (EK Success); threads (Me & My Big Ideas); metal charm (Card Connection); number buttons (Junkitz); pink wooden frame (Li'l Davis Designs); safety pins; ribbons; black and white cardstocks; white acrylic paint

Alyson Kristine Howe

A verse from a favorite song said it all for Amy, who created this quietly sweet layout to match the dreams of her little one. Ribbons and pastel rivets and tacks add baby-soft charm.

Amy Howe, Frisco, Texas

Supplies: Patterned papers, love tile and border strip die cuts, stickers, rivets, tacks and textured cardstock (Chatterbox); ribbon (Making Memories, Offray); library card (Jest Charming); gold stamping ink; pen; paint

Delight in the Little Things

Parents delight in watching their children sleep, as Sheila demonstrates in this layout of her son off to dreamland. She used image-editing software to alter her photographs, adjusting the hue and saturation to coordinate with her papers.

Sheila Toppi, Lowell, Massachusetts

Supplies: Patterned papers, frame, borders, letter stickers and die cuts (K & Company); deco square punches (Family Treasures); frog and dragonfly punches (McGill)

Victoria Elizabeth

Blocks of pastel colors form a serene backdrop of a photo of baby Victoria. Nancy crumpled, ironed and sanded the paper strips, then inked around the edges. Vellum printed with journaling overlays the background, allowing the colors to show through.

Nancy Rogers, Baton Rouge, Louisiana

Supplies: Patterned papers (Mustard Moon); ribbons (Making Memories); buttons (Jesse James); vellum (DMD); shadow ink (Hero Arts); embroidery floss; white cardstock

I Love You Biona

Jennifer embraced this moment of baby Fiona awakening to big sister's kiss, playing up the fact that her older daughter calls the baby "Biona." She machine stitched squiggly lines across the bottom of the page for a whimsical look that matches her title.

Jennifer Bucheli, Minneola, Florida

Supplies: Patterned paper and die-cut tags (SEI); peach and natural cardstocks; buttons; date stamp; black stamping ink; sewing machine

That's My Boy

Melodee clothed this page in soft yet boyish elements. She scanned and printed her son's actual pajamas on a transparency, then cut out and adhered the "03" to the canvas pocket to symbolize his age, the baseball theme and bedtime. A large satin ribbon placed across the layout draws attention to her son's silk-trimmed security blanket.

Melodee Langworthy, Rockford, Michigan

Supplies: Patterned papers (Autumn Leaves, Sticker Studio); printed transparency (Creative Imaginations); canvas pocket (Li'l Davis Designs); twill (7 Gypsies); ribbon (Offray); eyelet snaps (K & Company); ruler sticker (EK Success); cream cardstock; buttons; brown stamping ink

A Young Lady Must…

Vanessa fell in love with these photos that seemed to show her daughter prepared for a grand adventure…but exhausted from the process! She journaled on paper plant stakes to point out various details in the photos.

Vanessa Spady, Virginia Beach, Virginia

Supplies: Patterned paper (Bo-Bunny Press); stickers (Heart & Home, Paper House Productions); heart embellishment (Card Connection); paper flowers (Hot Off The Press); tin tiles (Making Memories); faux wax seal (Creative Imaginations); measure tape sticker (EK Success); tassel and curly clips (Target); paper plant stakes (Boxer Scrapbook Productions); zipper (Junkitz); white and red cardstocks; red, brown and black stamping inks; black pen

Beautiful Dreamer

This sleeping beauty dances off to slumber on a layout Natalie designed around her daughter's ballet costume. She printed her title on glossy photo paper, using white type in a black text box to coordinate with sheer black ribbons and her daughter's tights.

Natalie Quandt, Rochester, Minnesota

Supplies: Decorative paper (Paper Company); ribbon (Making Memories); flower charm (Card Connection); black cord (source unknown); black and white cardstocks; photo paper; vellum; brads; chalk

T is for Teatime

tea•time (tê´ tīm´) n. the time of day when tea is customarily served

WHO: Ryen M.
WHAT: 5th Birthday
WHERE: at Ryen's
WHEN: Dec 7, 2003
WHY: To have a birthday tea party!

Tea Party

A two-page spread was the proper format for showcasing all six photos from Janett's daughter's tea party. By adjusting the photos' sizes, she kept the layout from appearing cluttered. A printed invitation provides the details of the event.

Janett McKee, Cedar Park, Texas

Supplies: Patterned papers (Carolee's Creations, KI Memories); number stencil (source unknown); maroon cardstock; black stamping ink

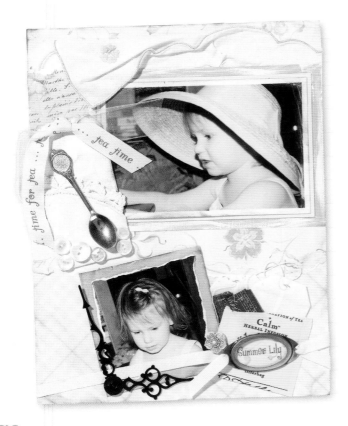

Teatime

While none of the photos from her daughter's tea party turned out as well as she had hoped, Ashley preserved the flavor of the event through soft colors and teatime ephemera. A miniature teaspoon and actual tea bags with packaging highlight the theme, while an old cotton napkin and lace handkerchief add nostalgic charm.

Ashley Calder, Dundas, Ontario, Canada

Supplies: Patterned papers (K & Company, PSX Design); metal label holder (Making Memories); flower button (Jesse James); buttons, clock hands, teaspoon, ribbons, cotton napkin, lace handkerchief; brown stamping ink; vellum

Teatime With Sierra

Sierra's tea party celebrates the beauty of being a girl, which Linda's design demonstrates. Using a stencil, Linda embossed heart images on vellum around the spread. Gold charms and letter stickers play up the sepia-toned photos.

Linda Cummings, Murfreesboro, Tennessee
Photos: Jennifer Torres for Classic Images, Nashville, Tennessee

Supplies: Patterned paper (NRN Designs); decorative vellum (Club Scrap); gold charms (Boutique Trims); letter stickers (EK Success); stencil (American Traditional Designs); fibers; white and pink cardstocks

Our Sweet Teas

The sweet enchantment of a childhood tea party comes to life on this layout. Sandi accented the spread with real tea bags and teatime embellishments, and created sugar cubes with embossing powder, extra thick embossing enamel and tiny glass marbles.

Sandi Minchuk, Merrillville, Indiana

Supplies: Patterned paper (Chatterbox); olive textured paper (Provo Craft); tag and teacup templates (Deluxe Designs); ribbon (May Arts); jewelry tags (American Tag); date stamp set (Making Memories); tiny glass marbles (JudiKins); spoon; teapot and teacup charms (Frost Creek Charms); fabric letters (Carolee's Creations); label maker (Dymo); extra thick embossing enamel; orange, tan and cream cardstocks; spoon; safety pins; staples; twine; hemp; bumpy textured paper; embossing powder; black stamping ink; chalk ink; walnut ink

Cup O' Joe

While playing with the hue saturation in image-editing software, Cherie brewed up this pop-art-style layout, percolating with color and whimsy. She printed the same photo multiple times in various colors to form a unique border.

Cherie Ward, Colorado Springs, Colorado

Supplies: Vellum (DieCuts with a View); image-editing software (Adobe Photoshop); mustard, blue, black, purple, brown, maroon, turquoise and white cardstocks; colored pencils

Well, maybe a caramel latte isn't exactly a cup of Joe, but what the heck. I love to wake up to a nice piping hot caramel latte. Naturally, nothing compliments a mug full of America's favorite caffeinated morning beverage like a homemade baked good. This of course quite decadent compared to what coffee used to be in our wonderful country. Coffee did simply start out as a cup of Joe, and we can thank our European friends for making coffee more than just a quick cup of percolated goodness with perhaps some sugar or cream. But, you may be asking yourself, "Where did the term, 'Cup of Joe,' come from?" Well, here is one possible origin. The U.S. Navy used to allow alcoholic beverages on U.S. Navy ships. Grog, ale, and beer were supplied in the general mess hall. When Admiral Josephus "Joe" Daniels became Chief of Naval Operations in 1913, he outlawed alcohol on board all ships, and ordered that coffee be served instead... hence the term "Cup of Joe." Now you know.

Amy's 7th birthday party was one of my all time favorites. We spent the summer before the party searching for unique cups and saucers at yard sales and we filled them with small treats to use as the party favors. Shannon Marie graciously let us have the party at her house as our tiny duplex couldn't hold 15 girls and 5 women. You girls were all so beautiful in your festive dresses and it was a delight to see the joy on your faces as we played games, decorated cookies and had a true tea party.

Nov. '97

AMY

A Tea Party Birthday

Cori painted on the backs of transparencies for an appearance much like smudges of cake frosting. She pierced patterned paper blocks and stitched them together for her background.

Cori Dahmen, Vancouver, Washington

Supplies: Patterned papers (Carolee's Creations); floral punches (Family Treasures); ribbon (May Arts); metal label holder (Magic Scraps); green, sage, pink and lavender cardstocks; transparency; thread; paint

One of the things that every child in Mrs. Joyce's grade 2 class look forward to is their turn to have Mischief the bear sleep over at their house. So needless to say Aysha was thrilled when it was her turn and she could introduce Mischief to Little Ted.

Little Ted was my favorite teddy bear and I have had him since I was a baby and always took him everywhere I went. Now he has been passed onto Aysha and he is her favorite teddy too. Because every morning he would end up on the floor and not on her bed where she left him, I had her convinced that he was really alive and would be up playing every night with her other toys. So when Mischief came over for his sleep over and Aysha was asleep I set up the floor of her room to look as if Little Ted and Mischief had been having a teddy bear's picnic during the night complete with food and drinks. When she got up in the morning she was so excited to see what they had been doing and thought that she had woken up too early and "caught them in the act" before they had the chance to climb back to where they had been when she had gone to bed! There is nothing quite like the innocence of childhood! Spring 2001

TEDDY BEARS Tea Party

Teddy Bears Tea Party

Trudy's daughter was thrilled when it was her turn to have the 2nd-grade class bear sleep over at her house. For the occasion, Trudy set up a tea party for the bear in secret. Painted wooden letters form the title, while tiny flower stickers and lace add dainty, feminine touches.

Trudy Sigurdson, Victoria, British Columbia, Canada

Supplies: Patterned papers, pink tag, molding and letter stickers (Chatterbox); wooden letters (Westrim); flower stickers (Jo-Ann Fabrics, Sandylion); mini tag (Office Depot); heart punch; cotton lace; silk flower; twill tape; pink eyelet; string; sewing machine

U is for Uh-Oh

uh-oh (u´ o´) interj. used to signify sudden awareness of a problem or error and the resulting worry

5 Staples

Shannon used staples as accents to document an unforgettable trip to the hospital. Clear glaze on the title letters give the page shine. Various number 5 embellishments were included to illustrate the number of staples in her son's head.

Shannon Taylor, Bristol, Tennessee

Supplies: Textured paper (Magic Scraps); staples and rub-ons (Making Memories); fabric, number tiles and zipper pulls (Junkitz); assorted "5's" (K & Company, Li'l Davis Designs, Me & My Big Ideas, Scrapworks); shadow-box frame (Pebbles); blue cardstock; domino; mini brad; thread; gauze; paint; clear glaze

Little Boy Boo Boos

Jen's photos and poem describe how a favorite toy can help comfort a child with a boo-boo. Gauze accents lend softness while appropriately fitting the page theme.

Jen Lowe, Lafayette, Colorado

Supplies: Patterned papers (Basic Grey); brads and clips (Creative Impressions); metal label holders (Li'l Davis Designs); slide mounts (Design Originals); Bingo placers and Scrabble tiles (Vintage); gauze; nailheads (source unknown); heart charm (source unknown)

Uh-oh!

Dimensional adhesive applied to Michelle's tag, label holder and title letters brings shimmer to this page about getting her daughter's cast off. The stamped twill border stitched to the page bears the words of the childhood game that caused the accident.

Michelle Pendleton, Colorado Springs, Colorado

Supplies: Patterned paper and sticker (Sweetwater); vellum, paper label holder, tag and journaling cardstock (Club Scrap); square mini brads (Creative Impressions); paper photo corners (3L); letter stamps (PSX Design, Stampendous); dimensional adhesive (Duncan); green and brick red cardstocks; cotton twill tape; thread; chalk; transparency; green chalk and black stamping inks; foam tape; muslin

Impatient

For her dynamic focal-point photo, Cori cut out the center of an 8 x 12" photo with a craft knife, matted it on torn cardstock, folded up the edges and stitched the mat in place. She punched a series of holes at the top of the photo and tied ribbons through for a saucy touch.

Cori Dahmen, Vancouver, Washington

Supplies: Die-cut letters (QuickKutz); ribbons (Li'l Davis Designs); metal word charm (Making Memories); jump ring (Darice); thread

Uh-oh, Spaghettio

Messy becomes a masterpiece on Valerie's layout, which uses circular tags, die cuts and various patterns to play up the Spaghetti-O theme. She chose papers with colors close to that of spaghetti sauce to dominate her design.

Valerie Barton, Flowood, Mississippi

Supplies: Patterned papers, tacks and circle die cut (Chatterbox); letter stamps and metal-rimmed circle tags (Making Memories); stickers (Mrs. Grossman's); mini tag (Scrappin' Extras); label maker labels (Dymo); safety pins; thread

V is for Vehicle

ve•hi•cle (ve´ hik´el) n. any device or contrivance for carrying or conveying persons or objects

Hummer

Monique highlighted her little one's big idea about receiving a Hummer for Christmas on this simple page. The round, metal-rimmed tags used for title letters repeat the circular shapes in the photo, while a strip of metallic paper contrasts with the stark background.

Monique McLean, Alabaster, Alabama

Supplies: Metallic paper (Magic Scraps); self-adhesive metal-rimmed tags and letter stickers (EK Success); label maker (Dymo); brown, black and tan cardstocks

Bring Out the Heavy Artillery

Sandra used found objects to adorn this page. She punched squares from four different security envelopes (the type in which bills arrive) to create a border. Silver hardware store tape links each square together.

Sandra Schmidt, Piesport, Germany

Supplies: Silver tape (Tyco Adhesives); letter stamps (Stamp Craft); metal circle clip (Target); silver fibers (DMC); silver ink; security envelopes; square punch; black cardstock

Road Rage

Mesh triangles in the corners of Sam's layout lend an industrial effect that plays nicely with her angled photos. New words her son says are listed on a metal-rimmed tag, as well as on the photos themselves with letter stickers.

Sam Cousins, Trumbull, Connecticut

Supplies: Patterned paper (K & Company); red mesh (Magic Mesh); stickers (Sticker Studio); charm letter and date photo turn (Making Memories); red fiber (Fibers By The Yard); metal rimmed tags (Staples); red acrylic paint

Old-Time Fun

When Mary's black-and-white photos came out with a greenish tint, she was disappointed at first, until she laid them next to this John Deere patterned paper! The green-inked windmill stamp on a green cardstock tag drives home the country-style essence of her spread.

Mary Faith Roell, Harrison, Ohio

Supplies: Patterned paper (Creative Imaginations); ribbon (Making Memories); letter stickers (Me & My Big Ideas); windmill stamp (source unknown); olive green mini brads; black, olive and dark green cardstocks; black and green stamping inks

Big Boys

Not wanting to stand in the way of the tire track pattern on her background paper, Tammy printed her title on a transparency so the pattern could roll through. She applied black ink on the metal accents for the effect of smeared grease.

Tammy Gauck, Jenison, Michigan

Supplies: Patterned paper (Karen Foster Design); snaps (Creative Imaginations); metal clip (7 Gypsies); black and blue cardstocks; transparency; black stamping ink

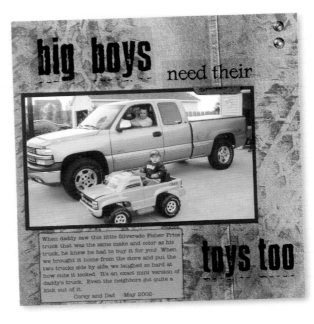

Monorail

Christine created a portal of fun on this layout by cutting apart a paper mat, adhering her focal-point photo inside, and then rolling and inking the edges. She punched holes on the left side of the page, running a cut and rolled paper strip and fibers between them.

Christine Traversa, Joliet, Illinois

Supplies: Patterned paper (Close To My Heart, Paper Loft); tag stickers (Pebbles); fibers (Rubba Dub Dub); decorative disc (Nunn Design); letter stickers (NRN Designs); clip hanger (www.scrapbugs.com); cocoa and teal stamping inks

Big Yellow Taxi

Brilliant yellows in the photos are boldly displayed against muted tones and soft stitching on Melissa's page of her daughter's free-wheeling fun. She layered her title words on one tag, creating a mini collage with an urban flair.

Melissa Chapman, Regina, Saskatchewan, Canada

Supplies: Patterned paper (Chatterbox, Provo Craft); tag (2DYE4); metal word and date stamp (Making Memories); metal label holder (www.twopeasinabucket.com); letter stamps (PSX Design); ribbon; pewter brad; tan, brown and white cardstocks; clear and caramel stamping inks; acrylic paint; sewing machine

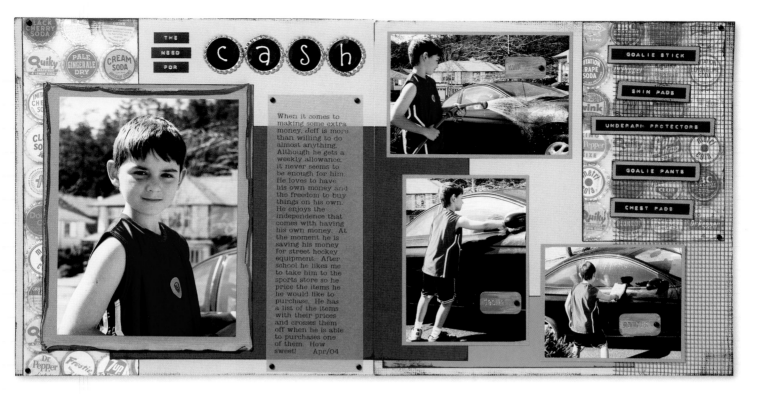

The Need for Cash

Lee records her son's desire for making extra money with photos of just one of his endeavors—washing cars. Label maker words matted on blue cardstock describe some of the items from his wish list of future purchases.

Lee Zwicker, Victoria, British Columbia, Canada

Supplies: Patterned paper (Rusty Pickle); metal dog tag words (Chronicle Books); wire mesh (Scrapyard 329); label maker labels (Dymo); bottle caps (Design Originals); letter stickers (Doodlebug Design); turquoise and light, medium and dark blue cardstocks; vellum; black stamping ink; brads; paint

Tricycle Repairing

Melodee worked with the letters and words in her patterned papers to expand upon her title and page theme. The red tile letters and bottle cap accents keep the page running smoothly in collaboration with the colors in the photos.

Melodee Langworthy, Rockford, Michigan

Supplies: Patterned papers (Mustard Moon); letter tiles and bottle caps (Li'l Davis Designs)

win•dow ga•zing (win´ dó gaz´ ing) v. looking out an opening in a building, often covered by glass

A Moment to Treasure

Laurel chose a rich, earthy color scheme to filter the warmth of the relationship in the focal-point photo onto the rest of the page. Hinges open the door to Laurel's hidden journaling printed on vellum.

Laurel Moser, Steinbach, Manitoba, Canada

Supplies: Patterned paper (7 Gypsies); letter stickers (K & Company, Pebbles, Sticker Studio); metallic word sticker (EK Success); letter stamps (PSX Design); ribbon (Offray); copper frame (K & Company); paper tag and hinges (Making Memories); fiber; brown and tan cardstocks; vellum; brown stamping ink

Fairies

Fantasy and frills adorn Colleen's layout that celebrates little girls. She hammered paper flower accents flat to reduce bulk, which add to the shabby chic feel of the page.

Colleen Macdonald, Winthrop, Australia

Supplies: Patterned paper (source unknown); fairy ephemera (www.alteredpages.com); keyhole accent, title letter pebbles and plates (Li'l Davis Designs); metal medallion (Beads and Plenty More); letter stickers (Colorbök, Creative Imaginations, Me & My Big Ideas); tiny letter stickers (Paper Fever); matte finish brads (Lasting Impressions); ribbon (Two Funky); tag and key (My Mind's Eye); button snaps (Cloud 9 Design); flowers (Michaels); cream and red cardstocks; black stamping ink

Daddy's Girl

Nicole played up the early morning shadows of her photo in her page design, using a craft knife to re-create the silhouette from black, gray and white cardstocks. A white pen to write the title was the only other supply used.

Nicole R. Amsler, Pfafftown, North Carolina

Supplies: Black, gray and white cardstocks; white pen

A Reflection of Youth

By tearing a space from an enlarged photo and inserting a strip of patterned paper in the space, Shandy created a unique spot for journaling. The layout is kept simple to focus on the view of the outside word.

Shandy Vogt, Nampa, Idaho

Supplies: Patterned paper (Chatterbox); letter sticker (Creative Imaginations); black and blue cardstocks

Daydreams

While watching her daughter gazing through a window deep in thought, Cathy saw a reflection of herself. She gave this layout timeless beauty with delicate paper ribbons, rhinestones and gold embellishments.

Cathy Lucas, Oro Valley, Arizona

Supplies: Black embossed paper, embossed vellum and embossed photo corners (K & Company); title template (Sizzix); paper heart ribbon (Close To My Heart); bow sticker and black rhinestones (Stampendous); metallic rub-ons (Craft-T); key and lock charms (Boutique Trims); wire; hand-printed sticker (Making Memories); cream bow and ribbon; heart charm; gold chain

Lucy 1 Year

To keep the focus on her photograph, Amy heat embossed gold powder around the edges of her photo mat. She sanded her patterned paper for an even softer look.

Amy Stultz, Mooresville, Indiana

Supplies: Patterned paper (Creative Imaginations); fiber (Fibers By The Yard); sticker (Magenta); heart button (source unknown); black stamping ink; gold embossing powder; black and olive cardstocks

On the Other Side

A game of peekaboo with her husband and son played from opposite sides of a window gave Desiree the opportunity to snap these photos. Rub-on words placed around a slide mount put young Gavin's expressions into words.

Desiree McClellan, Decatur, Alabama

Supplies: Patterned paper (Doodlebug Design); letter stickers (Sticker Studio); rub-ons (Making Memories); slide mount; vellum; tan and brown cardstocks; black stamping ink

Reflejos

Patricia documented how her son would stand at the front window waiting for his father to come home at just 10 months old. Her title, meaning "reflections" in French, is a combination of metal letters and premade cut-outs.

Patricia Jacoulot, Issy Les Moulineaux, Hauts de Seine, France

Supplies: Patterned papers (Magenta, Provo Craft); silver mesh (Magic Mesh); shaped clips, metal letters and metal star (Making Memories); letter cut-outs and vellum (Hot Off The Press); light orange and black cardstocks; black chalk stamping ink

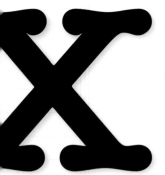

X is for X-traordinary

ex•traor•di•nar•y (ik stror´ dn er´ e) n. exceptional to a high degree; noteworthy; remarkable

Xtraordinary

Samantha eliminated the boundaries of her photo by sponging on three shades of brown ink, then applying gesso around the photograph and painting it with watercolors once the gesso dried. She cut out an "X" from metal, then sanded and painted it with gesso and green watercolors. Half of her smaller metal letters were also painted with gesso and green paint.

Samantha Walker, Battle Ground, Washington

Supplies: Gesso (Grumbacher); decorative brads, eyelets and eyelet letters (Making Memories); watercolor paints (Winsor & Newton); tan, blue and brown cardstocks; metal sheet; vellum; thread; brown stamping inks; black pen

Y is for Yell and Yawn

yawn (yon) v. to open mouth and breathe deeply; result of fatigue, drowsiness or boredom
yell (yel) v. to cry out loudly; shriek; scream

Laurelei

Heidi accented key words in her journaling through hand-stitching. She used a template to punch the letter holes onto cardstock and into corkboard, and then did a backstitch around the holes to form the letters.

Heidi Schueller, Waukesha, Wisconsin

Supplies: Patterned paper (Flair Designs); classic letter template and fibers (Timeless Touches); tan cardstock; paper piercer; corkboard; buttons; 24-gage embroidery needle

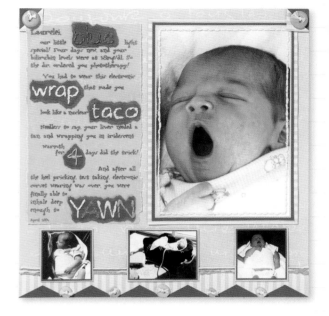

Lullabye Time

Like a baby dozing off to sleep, Jeniece's stamped title fades into the background of patterned papers behind it. She sanded the top of blue embossed paper, revealing dots outlined in white.

Jeniece Higgins, Lake Forest, Illinois

Supplies: Patterned paper and letter sticker (SEI); music paper, photo corners and charm (Provo Craft); letter stamps and ribbon (Li'l Davis Designs); date stamp (Making Memories); calendar page; notebook paper; burlap; sandpaper; black stamping ink; sewing machine; brown pen

Yawn 7:48

Kelli used a photo of her son yawning over his homework to illustrate a page about his busy schedule. Colored squares of paper divide his day into orderly blocks of time.

Kelli Noto, Centennial, Colorado

Supplies: Blue, light blue, yellow, green, orange, red and cream cardstocks